150 Best Recipes for
Cooking in
Foil

150 Best Recipes for Cooking in Foil

Ovens • BBQ • Camping

Marilyn Haugen

Robert
ROSE

For complete cataloguing information, see page 208.

Disclaimer
The recipes in this book have been carefully tested by our kitchen and our tasters. To the best of our knowledge, they are safe and nutritious for ordinary use and users. For those people with food or other allergies, or who have special food requirements or health issues, please read the suggested contents of each recipe carefully and determine whether or not they may create a problem for you. All recipes are used at the risk of the consumer.

We cannot be responsible for any hazards, loss or damage that may occur as a result of any recipe use.

For those with special needs, allergies, requirements or health problems, in the event of any doubt, please contact your medical adviser prior to the use of any recipe.

Design and production: Daniella Zanchetta/PageWave Graphics Inc.
Editor: Sue Sumeraj
Recipe editor: Jennifer MacKenzie
Proofreader: Sheila Wawanash
Indexer: Gillian Watts

Cover photograph:
Photographer: Colin Erricson
Associate photographer: Matt Johannsson
Food stylist: Michael Elliott
Prop stylist: Charlene Erricson

Interior photographs:
Photography: Tango Photography
Food stylist: Éric Régimbald
Accessory stylist: Véronique Gagnon-Lalanne

Illustrations: Kveta/threeinabox.com

Cover image: Zesty Cilantro Lime Grilled Chicken (page 94)

The publisher gratefully acknowledges the financial support of our publishing program by the Government of Canada through the Canada Book Fund.

Published by Robert Rose Inc.
120 Eglinton Avenue East, Suite 800, Toronto, Ontario, Canada M4P 1E2
Tel: (416) 322-6552 Fax: (416) 322-6936
www.robertrose.ca

Printed and bound in Canada

1 2 3 4 5 6 7 8 9 MI 24 23 22 21 20 19 18 17 16

Contents

Introduction

When I was first approached about writing a cookbook that included camping recipes, I was skeptical. I am not a camper and had vague memories of some strange concoctions we made as young Girl Scouts. What did intrigue me was the potential for making easy, moist and delicious one-container meals for both the grill and the oven. After all, who doesn't like meals that are infused with flavor and easy to clean up afterwards?

My daughter loves to go camping with friends, and since she has always been one of my most brutally honest taste-testers, I knew she would be a great help with the camping recipes. I also have several friends who are campers — some rugged campers, some home-away-from-home campers. They were all excited about the idea of trying out new recipes and giving me suggestions and hints for perfect camping meals.

I was personally enthusiastic about foil-wrapped oven meals, and my dear friend Karla Rabusch was eager to help me out with those recipes. I knew busy professionals and families would appreciate how quickly and effortlessly these meals could be put together.

As for the grilling recipes, the beauty of foil-wrapped meals is that it is much easier to get moist, flavorful results — you no longer have the age-old worry about your food drying out as it cooks on the grill. These recipes are also fantastic for those diehard sports fans who love to host tailgate parties.

Some of the recipes in this book are traditionally prepared in foil packets, and I've given you clear-cut instructions for the best results. Others are based on recipes that typically receive a different preparation but are updated to work brilliantly in foil wrap. All of the recipes use ingredients you are likely to have on hand, and very little cleanup is required. For recipes that are intended to be made away from home, I chose ingredients that can be stored and transported easily and — particularly for camping — that can be used in a variety of dishes.

So, with all these things going for us, let's get started with foil-wrapped cooking!

— *Marilyn Haugen*
www.foodthymes.com

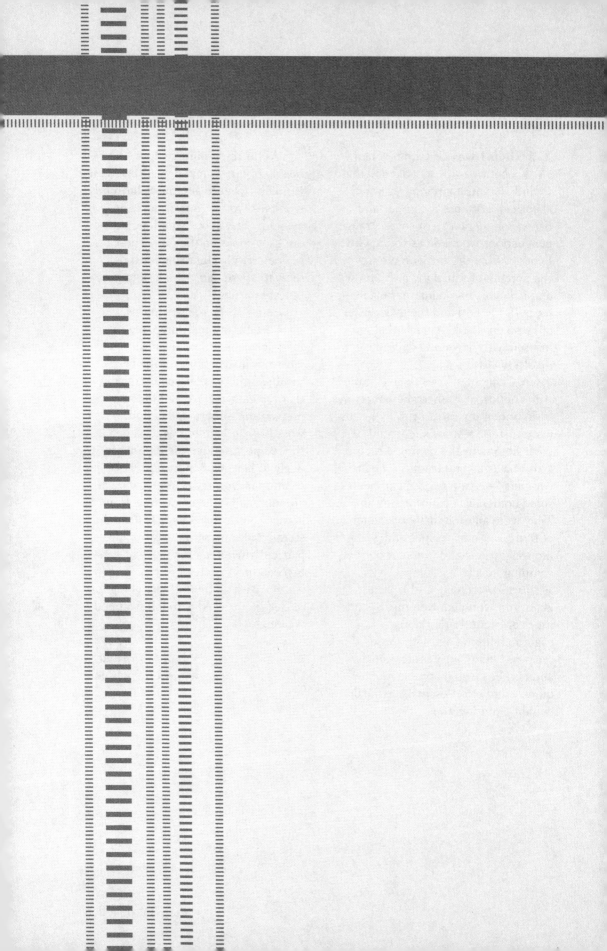

Getting Started

You will need 18-inch (45 cm) or 12-inch (30 cm) wide heavy-duty foil for these recipes. For each packet, you will use sheets of foil that are 18 by 12 inches (45 by 30 cm) unless otherwise noted in the recipe. In many cases, you will want to use double or triple layers of foil for the best results; each recipe indicates how many layers you need. Spray the top layer with nonstick cooking spray to prevent sticking.

After you arrange the ingredients in the center of the foil as directed in the recipe, you will wrap the foil around the ingredients in one of two ways:

- **Flat packets:** These are folded tightly against the ingredients on all sides. Flat packets are best suited for foods that you want to brown, rather than steam.

- **Tent-style packets:** These are folded so as to leave an air pocket over the ingredients, to allow steam to circulate during cooking. They are still tightly sealed on all sides. Tent-style packets are best suited for recipes made with vegetables or fruits or topped with cheese.

Each recipe tells you which packet style to use, and the steps and illustrations on pages 10–11 show you exactly how to make the packets. How simple is that?

Other Handy Equipment

Aside from the heavy-duty foil and nonstick cooking spray, there are just a few other tools that will help make your foil-wrapped meals a success.

For a Campfire

- A heavy-duty cooler or refrigerator that keeps ingredients below 40°F (4°C).

- A heated campfire with a grate. In some recipes, the packets are placed directly on the coals, while others require a grate. The coals should be just starting to turn white, with no flames, for the medium heat required for these recipes. When an adult can hold a hand comfortably about 6 inches (15 cm) above the coals for 3 to 4 seconds, the coals are at an ideal heat.

- Silicone-coated tongs for transferring the packets to and from the campfire.

For Grilling

- Any standard gas or charcoal barbecue grill with a cover.

- A heavy-duty cooler or refrigerator that keeps ingredients below 40°F (4°C) if you are transporting ingredients away from home for grilling.

- Silicone-coated tongs and a rimless baking sheet for transferring packets to and from the grill.

How to Make a Flat Packet

1. Place the ingredients in the center of the foil as directed in the recipe.

2. Bring the long ends of the foil together over the ingredients and fold the foil down until it is tight against the ingredients.

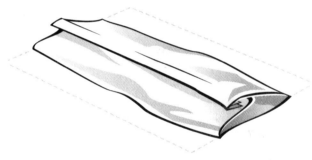

3. Fold up each open end of the foil until the folds are tight against the ingredients and the packet is sealed tightly.

How to Make a Tent-Style Packet

1. Place the ingredients in the center of the foil as directed in the recipe.

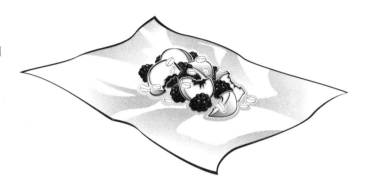

2. Bring the long ends of the foil together over the ingredients and fold the foil down until the top of the packet is sealed tightly but there is a substantial gap between the food and the top of the packet.

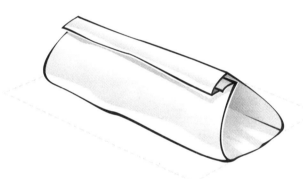

3. Fold up each open end of the foil until the folds are tight against the ingredients and the sides of the packet are sealed tightly.

For the Oven

- A baking sheet to make it easy to transfer the packets into and out of the oven.

- A food processor for recipes in which ingredients are finely chopped or sauces are blended.

Food for Camping

The camping recipes use canned ingredients or pantry staples that are easy to pack along. The same basic seasonings, such as table salt, ground black pepper and dried herbs, are used in many recipes so that you only need to pack a few seasonings. Feel free to substitute your favorite seasonings if you have the storage room or prefer more gourmet seasonings.

Some of the recipes can be prepared ahead of time at home, refrigerated or frozen, and then cooked at your campsite.

When packing your cooler and pantry staples, organize your ingredients so that the items you won't be using until later in your trip are at the bottom and the ones you'll be using first are at the top. Pack items you will be accessing frequently, such as drinks, in other containers so you are not constantly opening the storage cooler and exposing longer-term storage items to warmer temperatures.

Safe Food Handling Tips

The following food safety advice is assembled and adapted from *Kitchen Companion: Your Safe Food Handbook*, a publication of the U.S. Department of Agriculture, Food Safety and Inspection Service.

General Guidelines

- Keep hot food hot and cold food cold. Whether you are in your kitchen or enjoying the great outdoors, there are some food safety principles that remain constant. The first is keeping food out of the "danger zone." Bacteria multiply rapidly at temperatures between 40°F and 140°F (4°C and 60°C). Never leave perishable food, whether hot or cold, in the danger zone for more than 2 hours (or 1 hour in temperatures above 90°F/32°C). This includes both hot food and cold food. If the food has been above 40°F (4°C) and below 140°F (60°C) more than 2 hours, discard it.

- Keep everything clean. Bacteria from raw meat and poultry products can easily spread to other foods via your hands or utensils or by juices dripping from packages. Always wash your hands before and after handling food, and use different platters and utensils for raw and cooked meat and poultry.

Transporting Food

- If you are traveling with cold food, a cooler is the key to keeping it out of the danger zone. Use an insulated cooler with enough ice or ice packs to keep the food at 40°F (4°C) or below. A block of ice lasts longer than ice cubes. Add the ice first, then the food. Pack an appliance thermometer in your cooler so you can monitor the temperature.

- It is difficult when traveling to keep hot food hot, so it's best to cook food before leaving home, then chill it in the refrigerator and transport it cold.

- When transporting raw meat or poultry, double-wrap the packages or place them in plastic bags to prevent juices from dripping on other foods. And pack them below other foods.

- Divide large amounts of food into shallow containers for fast chilling and easier use. Keep cooked food refrigerated until it's time to leave home, then pack it straight from the refrigerator into the cooler.

- Take foods in the smallest quantity you are likely to need.

- Remember your food thermometer! Meat and poultry cooked on a grill or campfire can brown quickly on the outside. Use the thermometer to be sure the food has reached a safe minimum internal temperature as indicated in the recipes.

- Soap and water are essential to cleanliness, so if you are going somewhere that will not have running water, bring water with you or have disposable wipes on hand.

At Your Destination

- Keep the cooler in the shade and insulate it with a blanket, tarp or poncho. Keep the lid closed and avoid repeated openings. Replenish the ice as it melts.

- Discard all used food packaging and bags. They could contaminate other food and cause foodborne illness, so don't reuse them.

Tips for Foil Packet Success

You will have the most success with cooking in foil if you keep the following guidelines in mind.

- Use heavy-duty foil and nonstick cooking spray.

- Prepare your packets according to the amounts specified in the recipe. Do not overstuff them.

- Avoid piercing or tearing your packets by using silicone-coated tongs to handle them and a baking sheet to help you transfer the packets to and from the grill or oven.

- Turn or rotate your packets as directed in the recipe, to avoid burning.

- Carefully open the packets after cooking to avoid burns caused by steam rising from the packets. Gently unfold the top and ends of each packet, allowing the steam to escape a little bit at a time. You can use oven mitts if you like, but they do make it a bit harder to open the seams.

Camping Recipes

Side Dishes

Desserts

Maple Walnut and Raisin–Stuffed Baked Apples

Makes 6 servings

An apple pouch filled with gooey granola, raisins and walnuts is a welcoming morning treat.

Tip

Cortland, Fuji, Jonagold, Honeycrisp and Granny Smith apples work exceptionally well in this recipe. If choosing another variety of apple, choose ones that have a firm flesh and are typically recommended for baking.

- Prepare campfire coals
- 6 sheets heavy-duty foil, sprayed with nonstick cooking spray

2 tbsp	butter, melted	30 mL
2 tbsp	pure maple syrup	30 mL
1 tsp	ground cinnamon	5 mL
½ cup	granola	125 mL
⅓ cup	raisins or dried cranberries	75 mL
¼ cup	finely chopped walnuts	60 mL
6	apples (see tip, at left)	6

1. In a medium bowl, combine butter, maple syrup and cinnamon. Add granola, raisins and walnuts, mixing well.

2. Cut tops off apples and cut out seeds, but leave bottoms intact. Place an apple on each prepared foil sheet. Pack granola mixture into the apples, dividing evenly. Fold edges of foil up into a bowl shape around the apple, then finish folding tightly in the flat packet style.

3. Bury packets in hot campfire ashes and cook for 30 to 35 minutes or until apples are soft.

Cinnamon Granola– Stuffed Pears

The combination of subtly sweet pears and crunchy granola makes this recipe a favorite for breakfast or dessert.

Tips

Plan ahead when using pears. Pears are always picked unripened and typically need about 7 days to fully ripen at home. To speed up ripening, place pears in a paper bag, seal the bag and store at room temperature, turning the bag occasionally. This step may shorten the ripening period by as much as 4 days.

Pears that are round, with a short stem, will give you more room for stuffing ingredients.

- Prepare campfire coals
- 2 sheets heavy-duty foil, sprayed with nonstick cooking spray

2	firm semisweet pears (such as Green Anjou or Bartlett)	2
2 tsp	packed light brown sugar	10 mL
2 tsp	butter	10 mL
¼ cup	granola	60 mL

1. Cut pears in half and scrape out centers. Place 2 halves on each prepared foil sheet. Add ½ tsp (2 mL) each brown sugar and butter in the center of each pear half, then add 1 tbsp (15 mL) granola. Fold foil into tent-style packets and seal edges tightly.

2. Place packets on hot coals and cook for 20 to 25 minutes or until pears are soft.

Variations

Add a pinch of ground cinnamon, nutmeg or cloves with the brown sugar for added flavor.

Omit the brown sugar and butter, and add ½ tsp (2 mL) liquid honey in the center of each pear half before the granola.

Add sunflower seeds or ground flax seeds (flaxseed meal) with the granola for some added punch.

Tropical Pineapple Donut Bundles

Makes 4 servings

Campers with a sweet tooth will delight in these simple-to-make, tempting breakfast treats.

Tips

Reserve the drained pineapple juice and combine it with orange juice for a delicious breakfast drink.

An 8-oz (227 mL) can of pineapple rings typically contains 4 rings. If your can has more, you can snack on the remainder while cooking, or cut them into chunks to serve with the bundles.

- Prepare campfire coals
- 4 sheets heavy-duty foil, sprayed with nonstick cooking spray

1	can (8 oz/227 mL) pineapple rings in juice, drained	1
3 tbsp	packed brown sugar	45 mL
3 tbsp	butter, softened	45 mL
2	large cake donuts, split in half	2

1. Place a donut half, cut side up, on each prepared foil sheet. In a small bowl or cup, combine brown sugar and butter; spread over cut side of donuts. Place a pineapple ring on top of each donut. Fold foil into tent-style packets and seal edges tightly.

2. Place packets on hot coals and cook for 5 to 7 minutes or until warmed through.

Variations

For a really moist and gooey donut, drizzle the drained pineapple juice on the donut before spreading on the butter mixture.

Before sealing the packets, top with maraschino cherries for a festive treat.

Sprinkle pineapple with shredded coconut before sealing the packets, for a piña colada–inspired treat.

Cranberry Muffins in Orange Cups

Show your young campers a little science experiment while camping. Everyone gets a kick out of the idea of baking muffins in orange shells.

Tip

Any of your favorite muffin mixes can be used in this recipe. Just make sure that water is the only ingredient you need to add.

• Prepare campfire coals
• 6 sheets heavy-duty foil, sprayed with nonstick cooking spray

| 6 | medium oranges | 6 |
| 1 | box just-add-water cranberry muffin mix (makes 6) | 1 |

1. Cut the top quarter off each orange. Using a spoon, scoop out pulp, pith and seeds, being careful to keep orange shell intact. Place 1 orange shell on each prepared foil sheet (reserve pulp for another use).

2. Prepare muffin mix according to package directions. Divide batter equally among orange shells, filling shells about two-thirds full. Wrap foil tightly around oranges, without covering the top opening.

3. Place packets on hot coals, making sure they cannot tip over, and cook for 10 to 15 minutes or until muffins tops are firm to the touch.

Toad in a Hole

This recipe is one of those old-time favorites that kids always like to watch you make. Now you can take them camping and enjoy the same tasty breakfast.

Tips

The holes in the sourdough can be cut out at home. Pack the cut-out bread and the holes in a sealable plastic bag.

If cutting the holes at the campsite, you can use the top of a drinking glass or an empty can.

Grill the sourdough holes until golden brown and serve with your favorite toast topping.

Any sturdy, thick-sliced bread can be used in place of the sourdough. Good examples are French bread or Texas toast.

- Prepare campfire coals
- 3-inch (7.5 cm) cookie or biscuit cutter
- 4 sheets heavy-duty foil, sprayed with nonstick cooking spray

4	thick slices sourdough bread	4
4	slices bacon, cut in half	4
4	large eggs	4
	Salt and ground black pepper	

1. Using the cookie cutter, cut a hole in the center of each slice of bread. Place 2 bacon halves in center of each prepared foil sheet. Top with 1 slice of bread. Crack an egg into each bread hole. Season with salt and pepper. Fold foil into tent-style packets and seal edges tightly.

2. Place packets on hot coals, making sure they are level, and cook for 7 to 10 minutes or until eggs are done to your liking.

Ham, Cheese and Egg Sandwiches

Just like your favorite on-the-go breakfast sandwich, this one is made outdoors with your choice of quality ingredients and without the hustle and bustle of the drive-through.

Tip

If you don't want your cheese melted, add the cheese slices on top of the eggs after removing the packets from the coals and before adding the English muffin tops.

- Prepare campfire coals
- 5 sheets heavy-duty foil, sprayed with nonstick cooking spray

4	English muffins, split in half	4
4	¼-inch (0.5 cm) thick slices ham or Canadian bacon	4
4	slices Cheddar or pepper Jack cheese	4
4	large eggs	4

1. For each packet, place an English muffin bottom in the center of a prepared foil sheet. Fold edges of foil up into a bowl shape around the muffin. Add a slice of ham and a slice of cheese. Crack an egg on top. Fold foil into a tent-style packet and seal edges tightly.

2. Place packets on hot coals, making sure they are level, and cook for 12 to 15 minutes or until eggs are done to your liking.

3. Meanwhile, place the English muffin tops on the remaining prepared foil sheet. Fold foil into a flat packet and seal edges tightly. Heat on coals for 7 to 9 minutes or until heated through.

4. Open each packet and top eggs with English muffin tops.

Hill Country Hash Brown Breakfast

||||||||||||||||||||||||||||||||||||||||||||||||||||||||||||||||||||||||||||||||||||||||||||||||||||||||||||||||||||||||||||||||||||||||||||||||||

Makes 6 servings

Start your day of camping off right with this hearty and satisfying all-in-one breakfast of diced potatoes, eggs and cheese, all piled on top of a breakfast sausage patty.

Tips

You can use regular diced hash brown potatoes instead of the O'Brien potatoes if you prefer. Or you can use a frozen hash brown patty.

Serve with a side of fresh fruit or fruit cups.

- Prepare campfire coals
- 6 sheets heavy-duty foil, sprayed with nonstick cooking spray

6	frozen cooked pork sausage patties, thawed	6
½	package (28 oz/796 g) frozen O'Brien hash brown potatoes, thawed	½
12	large eggs, whisked	12
	Salt and ground black pepper	
1	package (8 oz/250 g) shredded Cheddar cheese	1

1. For each serving, place a sausage patty on a prepared foil sheet. Top with ⅔ cup (150 mL) hash browns. Fold edges of foil up into a bowl shape around the patty. Divide eggs evenly among packets. Season to taste with salt and pepper. Fold foil into tent-style packets and seal edges tightly.

2. Place packets on hot coals, making sure they are level, and cook for 10 to 12 minutes or until sausage and potatoes are heated through and eggs are set. Open packets with caution, allowing steam to escape, and divide cheese evenly among packets. Return packets to coals and cook for 3 to 5 minutes or until cheese is melted to your liking.

Variations

Finely chop 1 tomato and divide it among the packets before adding the cheese.

A thin slice of ham or Canadian bacon is a delicious substitute for the sausage patty.

Hearty Sausage and Egg Breakfast

This simple, classic breakfast of sausage, eggs and hash browns is immensely satisfying and a great way to start your day of camping activities.

Tip

Before adding the eggs to the packet, make sure to fold the foil up so the eggs do not run out.

- Prepare campfire coals
- 2 sheets heavy-duty foil, sprayed with nonstick cooking spray

2	frozen hash brown patties, thawed	2
4	large eggs, whisked	4
2	frozen cooked sausage patties, thawed	2
	Salt and ground black pepper	
	Pure maple syrup (optional)	

1. Place a hash brown patty on each prepared foil sheet. Fold edges of foil up into a bowl shape around the patty. Divide eggs evenly between packets. Top each with a sausage patty. Season to taste with salt and pepper. Fold foil into tent-style packets and seal edges tightly.

2. Place packets on hot coals, making sure they are level, and cook for 10 to 12 minutes or until hash brown and sausage patties are heated through and eggs are cooked to your liking.

Variation

Substitute frozen waffles for the hash brown patties.

Lumberjack Breakfast

||||||||||||||||||||||||||||||||||||||||||||||||||||||||||||||||||||||||||||||||||||||||||||||||||||||||||||||||||||||||||||||||||||||||||||

Makes 1 serving

These breakfast packets make a deep woods–worthy breakfast that will satisfy a hungry bunch of campers. I have written the recipe for one serving so that each camper can assemble their own individualized version (see variations).

Tips

Use caution when opening the foil packet, as the escaping steam is very hot.

Serve with a side of fresh fruit or fruit cups.

- Prepare campfire coals
- 1 sheet heavy-duty foil, sprayed with nonstick cooking spray

1	slice Canadian bacon	1
¼ cup	frozen hash browns, thawed	60 mL
1	large egg	1
¼ cup	chopped tomatoes	60 mL
3 tbsp	shredded Cheddar cheese	45 mL
	Salt and ground black pepper	

1. Place Canadian bacon on prepared foil sheet. Fold edges of foil up into a bowl shape around the bacon. Add hash browns, then crack the egg over the potatoes. Top with tomatoes. Fold foil into a tent-style packet and seal edges tightly.

2. Place packet on hot coals, making sure it is level, and cook for 15 minutes. Open packets with caution, allowing steam to escape, and add cheese. Return packet to coals and cook for 3 to 5 minutes or until cheese is melted to your liking. Season to taste with salt and pepper.

Variations

For a vegetarian version, simply omit the bacon or replace it with sliced zucchini or yellow summer squash.

Add hot pepper sauce, Cajun seasoning or hot pepper flakes if you like a kick.

Add thinly sliced green onions, finely chopped onions or finely chopped green bell peppers with the tomatoes.

Ready-to-Go Breakfast Tacos

||||||||||||||||||||||||||||||||||||||||||||||||||||||||||||||||||||||||||||||||||||||||||||||||||||||||||||||||||||||||||||||||||||

These make-ahead breakfast tacos are full of flavor and provide a hearty meal to start the day. They're so good, you'll want to have them on hand for daily breakfasts at home, too.

Tips

Defrost your corn in the refrigerator or cooler, not at room temperature.

For warm tortillas, spray 1 large foil sheet with cooking spray. Stack tortillas 2 at a time, separating each pair with a sheet of parchment paper. Fold foil into a flat packet and seal edges tightly. Heat on coals for 5 to 7 minutes, turning packets over once, until warm.

Store the packets in a cooler at 40°F (4°C) until ready to cook. Thaw frozen tacos in the cooler (or refrigerator) before cooking.

- 6 double sheets heavy-duty foil, top sheets sprayed with nonstick cooking spray

Make Ahead

6	cooked pork sausage links, cut into ½-inch (1 cm) pieces	6
2	jalapeño peppers, seeded and thinly sliced	2
2	red bell peppers, thinly sliced	2
1	small red onion, thinly sliced	1
1	can (14 oz/398 mL) black beans, drained (1½ cups/375 mL)	1
1 cup	frozen corn, thawed	250 mL
½ cup	salsa	125 mL
2 tbsp	olive oil	30 mL
1 tsp	kosher salt	5 mL
1 tsp	ground coriander	5 mL
½ tsp	freshly ground black pepper	2 mL

At the Campsite

6	large eggs	6
	Salt and ground black pepper	
½ cup	shredded Monterey Jack cheese	125 mL
12	taco-size (8-inch/20 cm) flour tortillas (see tip, at left)	12

Make Ahead

1. In a large bowl, combine sausages, jalapeños, red peppers, onion, beans, corn, salsa, oil, salt, coriander and pepper.

2. Divide sausage mixture evenly among prepared foil sheets. Fold foil into tent-style packets and seal edges tightly. Refrigerate for up to 2 days or freeze for up to 1 month.

At the Campsite

3. Prepare campfire coals. Place packets on hot coals and cook for 7 to 10 minutes, moving packets occasionally, until sausage mixture is very hot.

4. Transfer packs to a flat surface and open with caution, allowing steam to escape. Crack 1 egg into the center of each packet. Season to taste with salt and pepper. Reseal packet, return to coals and cook for 4 to 6 minutes or until eggs are done to your liking. Serve sprinkled with cheese, with 2 tortillas per packet.

Make-Ahead Breakfast Burritos

These filling, delicious burritos are the perfect breakfast or brunch for camping trips because they can be fully prepared ahead of time and then just cooked on site until heated through.

Tip

Double the recipe for larger groups or to have these on hand for an easy breakfast on busy days.

Variations

Use frozen O'Brien hash brown potatoes for the added flavor of onions and green bell peppers.

Substitute another semi-hard cheese, such as Colby or mild Cheddar, for the Monterey Jack.

• 8 sheets heavy-duty foil, sprayed with nonstick cooking spray

1 lb	pork sausage (bulk or casing removed)	500 g
½	package (16 oz/454 g) frozen diced hash brown potatoes	½
8	large eggs	8
¼ cup	sour cream	60 mL
	Salt and ground black pepper	
	Nonstick cooking spray (optional)	
8 oz	shredded Monterey Jack cheese	250 g
8	burrito-size (10-inch/25 cm) flour tortillas	8

Make Ahead

1. In a large skillet, cook sausage over medium heat, breaking it up with a spoon, for 5 to 7 minutes or until no longer pink. Drain, transfer to a large bowl and set aside.

2. Cook potatoes according to package directions.

3. Meanwhile, in a large bowl, whisk eggs. Whisk in sour cream. Season to taste with salt and pepper.

4. Spray skillet with cooking spray, if needed to coat bottom of skillet. Heat over medium-high heat, add egg mixture and cook, stirring, for 3 to 5 minutes or until eggs are done to your liking.

5. Add potatoes, eggs and cheese to the sausage, stirring to combine. Let cool completely.

6. For each burrito, place a tortilla on a flat surface and add about ⅓ cup (75 mL) of the sausage mixture in the center. Fold in bottom and top edges of tortilla and roll up sides. Place burrito, seam side down, on a prepared foil sheet. Wrap foil tightly around burrito and seal edges tightly. Freeze burritos for up to 3 weeks.

At the Campsite

7. Prepare campfire coals. Place packets on hot coals and cook for 7 to 12 minutes or until heated through.

Pepper Jack, Corn and Mushroom Quesadillas

These vegetarian quesadillas have just the right amount of melted cheese, and the little bit of spice makes them totally delectable.

Tips

You can substitute 2 cups (500 mL) frozen corn kernels, thawed, for the canned corn.

If you would prefer less spicy quesadillas, use Monterey Jack cheese instead of pepper Jack.

• 2 sheets heavy-duty foil, sprayed with nonstick cooking spray

2 tsp	olive oil	10 mL
1	small red onion, thinly sliced	1
8 oz	mushrooms, thinly sliced	250 g
1	can (14 oz/398 mL) corn kernels, drained	1
	Salt and ground black pepper	
4	taco-size (8-inch/20 cm) flour tortillas	4
1¼ cups	shredded pepper Jack cheese	300 mL

Make Ahead

1. In a medium skillet, heat oil over medium heat. Add onion and mushrooms; cook, stirring, for 7 to 9 minutes or until softened and moisture released from mushrooms has evaporated. Stir in corn, remove from heat and let cool. Season to taste with salt and pepper.

2. For each quesadilla, place a tortilla on a prepared foil sheet. Sprinkle with one-quarter of the cheese. Top with half the corn mixture, then sprinkle with another quarter of the cheese. Place another tortilla on top. Fold foil into a flat packet and seal edges tightly. Refrigerate for up to 5 days.

At the Campsite

3. Prepare campfire coals, with grate set on top. Place packets on grate and cook for 3 minutes. Turn packets over and cook for 2 to 3 minutes or until cheese is melted and tortillas are crisp.

Variation

Add diced jalapeño peppers with the onion, and/or add diced black olives or thinly sliced green onions with the corn. Added ingredients should not exceed ¼ cup (60 mL) so as not to overfill the quesadillas.

Catch of the Day with Brown Rice and Zucchini

Makes 4 servings

This dish is a fun one to make campside with your freshly caught fish. Kids especially love the experience of cooking their catch of the day. It doesn't get much fresher than that.

Tips

Substitute your catch of the day for the trout. Measure your fish at the thickest point. Fish should be cooked for about 15 minutes per inch (2.5 cm) of thickness. Fish less than 1 inch (2.5 cm) thick do not need to be turned during cooking and can be cooked for 10 to 12 minutes.

You can replace the fresh basil with 4 tsp (20 mL) dried.

The packets can be assembled up to 4 hours before cooking. Keep refrigerated or in a cooler below 40°F (4°C).

- Prepare campfire coals
- 4 sheets heavy-duty foil, sprayed with nonstick cooking spray

1	zucchini, thinly sliced	1
1 lb	trout fillet, cut into 4 pieces	500 g
2 cups	cooked brown rice	500 mL
¼ cup	loosely packed fresh basil leaves, thinly sliced	60 mL
1 cup	cherry tomatoes, halved	250 mL
¼ cup	Italian dressing	60 mL

1. Arrange zucchini slices in a single layer on prepared foil sheets, dividing evenly. Place fish on top of zucchini. Add rice around fish, dividing evenly. Top fish with basil and tomatoes. Drizzle with dressing. Fold foil into tent-style packets and seal edges tightly.

2. Place packets on hot coals and cook for 12 to 15 minutes, turning packets over once, until fish flakes easily when tested with a fork.

Sweet-and-Spicy Tuna Melts

This recipe imbues the classic tuna melt sandwich with sweet pickle relish and hot sauce for a sweet-and-spicy flavor that will knock your socks off.

Tip

The tuna mixture can be stored in an airtight container in the refrigerator for up to 2 days.

• Prepare campfire coals
• 6 sheets heavy-duty foil, sprayed with nonstick cooking spray

2	cans (each 6 oz/170 g) water-packed packed tuna, drained	2
1 cup	finely chopped celery	250 mL
½ cup	finely chopped onion	125 mL
1½ tsp	Sriracha (or to taste)	7 mL
3 tbsp	sweet pickle relish	45 mL
1 cup	shredded Cheddar cheese, divided	250 mL
¼ cup	mayonnaise	60 mL
3	English muffins, split in half	3
6	slices tomato (optional)	6
	Salt and ground black pepper	

1. In a large bowl, combine tuna, celery, onion, Sriracha and relish. Fold in ¼ cup (60 mL) cheese and mayonnaise until well combined.

2. Place an English muffin half on each prepared foil sheet. Spread tuna mixture on top, dividing evenly. Sprinkle with the remaining cheese, dividing evenly. Fold foil into tent-style packets and seal edges tightly.

3. Place packets on hot coals and cook for 7 to 10 minutes or until warmed through and cheese is melted. Open packets with caution, allowing steam to escape, and, if desired, top with tomato slices. Season to taste with salt and pepper.

Creamy Chicken and Broccoli Packets

You will love how easy, delicious and satisfying this comfort food feast is. I've included the oven method in a tip, because I know you will want to make this again and again.

Tip

To make this dish at home, preheat the oven to 400°F (200°C). Prepare the packets as described in step 1. Place packets in middle of oven and cook for 30 to 35 minutes or until an instant-read thermometer inserted in the thickest part of a chicken breast registers 165°F (74°C). Remove packets from oven and let stand for 5 minutes before opening. If desired, you can put the packets on a baking sheet to make it easier to transfer them into and out of the oven.

- Prepare campfire coals
- 6 sheets heavy-duty foil, sprayed with nonstick cooking spray

1	package (6 oz/175 g) stuffing mix	1
1½ cups	water	375 mL
6	boneless skinless chicken breasts (about 1½ lbs/750 g), pounded to ½ inch (1 cm) thick	6
4 cups	broccoli florets	1 L
1½ cups	shredded Cheddar cheese	375 mL
3	slices bacon, cooked crisp and crumbled	3
½ cup	ranch dressing	125 mL

1. In a large bowl, combine stuffing and water. Spoon stuffing onto prepared foil sheets, dividing evenly. Place chicken breasts on top. Add broccoli, cheese and bacon, dividing evenly. Drizzle with dressing. Fold foil into tent-style packets and seal edges tightly.

2. Place packets on hot coals and cook for 25 to 30 minutes or until an instant-read thermometer inserted horizontally into the thickest part of a chicken breast registers 165°F (74°C). Remove packets from coals and let stand for 5 minutes before opening.

Honey Mustard Chicken and Potato Packets

Makes 4 servings

The honey mustard coating the chicken livens this dish. Paired with seasoned O'Brien potatoes, the meal becomes extra-special.

Tips

When checking the temperature of the chicken, be careful not to pierce the bottom of the packet.

Open packets carefully, allowing steam to escape, when checking doneness. Reseal packets and return to coals, if needed..

- Prepare campfire coals
- 4 sheets heavy-duty foil, sprayed with nonstick cooking spray

1 tbsp	liquid honey	15 mL
3 tbsp	Dijon mustard	45 mL
4	boneless skinless chicken breasts (about 1 lb/500 g)	4
1	package (16 oz/454 g) frozen diced O'Brien potatoes, thawed	1
	Seasoning salt	

1. In a sealable plastic bag, combine honey and mustard. Add chicken, seal bag and toss to coat.

2. Divide potatoes evenly among prepared foil sheets. Season with seasoning salt. Using tongs, transfer chicken breasts to top potatoes. Drizzle with any excess honey mustard mixture. Fold foil into tent-style packets and seal edges tightly.

3. Place packets on hot coals and cook for 15 to 20 minutes, turning packets over once halfway through, until an instant-read thermometer inserted in the thickest part of a chicken breast registers 165°F (74°C).

Apricot Chicken with Sriracha Lime Sauce

Makes 4 servings

The sweet and sour flavors in this chicken dish combine for an explosion of delectable flavors. Change up the frozen vegetables you use, and you have a dish you can make often without feeling like it is the same old dish.

Tip

Use an Asian-inspired stir-fry vegetable mix, such as a bell pepper mix, an asparagus mix or a broccoli, carrot and water chestnut mix. A mix that features carrots, cauliflower florets and green beans will also complement this dish wonderfully.

- Prepare campfire coals
- 4 sheets heavy-duty foil, sprayed with nonstick cooking spray

1	package (16 oz/500 g) frozen mixed vegetables (see tip, at left), thawed	1
1⅓ cups	apricot preserves	325 mL
2 tbsp	soy sauce	30 mL
2 tbsp	lime juice	30 mL
2 tsp	Sriracha	10 mL
	Salt and ground black pepper	
4	boneless skinless chicken breasts (about 1 lb/500 g)	4

1. In a small bowl, combine preserves, soy sauce, lime juice and Sriracha. Season to taste with salt and pepper.

2. Place a chicken breast on each prepared foil sheet. Add 2 tbsp (30 mL) apricot sauce on top of each breast. Add vegetables on top of and around each breast, dividing evenly. Top with the remaining apricot sauce, dividing evenly. Fold foil into tent-style packets and seal edges tightly.

3. Place packets on hot coals and cook for 15 to 20 minutes or until an instant-read thermometer inserted in the thickest part of a chicken breast registers 165°F (74°C).

Variation

Combine 2 cups (500 mL) cooked rice (any variety) and 2 cups (500 mL) water. Let stand for 5 minutes, then drain and add rice to packets with the vegetables, dividing evenly.

Chicken Thighs with Cinnamon-Braised Carrots and Apples

||||||||||||||||||||||||||||||||||||||||||||||||||||||||||||||||||||||||||||||||||||||||||||||||||||||||||||||||||||||||||||

The only difficult thing about this dinner is waiting for it to be done when you are smelling the amazing aromas floating from your campfire. But it only gets better when you open the packets and see the beautifully glazed carrots and apples and the grilled chicken.

Tips

To debone chicken thighs, use a paring or boning knife to cut a line through the meat along both sides of the bone. Expose the bone, scraping away any small pieces of meat. When the meat has been mostly scraped off the bone, separate the end of the bone from the meat. Trim off any leftover bone or gristle still on the thigh. Chicken can be very slippery, so curl your fingers when cutting to avoid exposing them to the knife.

To test if the chicken is cooked, carefully open one packet, allowing the steam to escape. Pierce the thigh with a knife. If the juices do not run clear, reseal the packet and continue to cook, retesting as needed.

- Prepare campfire coals
- 4 sheets heavy-duty foil, sprayed with nonstick cooking spray

3	apples (such as Fuji), peeled and thinly sliced	3
2 tbsp	granulated sugar	30 mL
½ tsp	ground cinnamon	2 mL
3 cups	baby carrots, cut in half lengthwise	750 mL
2 tbsp	dried parsley	30 mL
2 tsp	dried thyme	10 mL
2 tsp	ground sage	10 mL
2	cloves garlic, minced	2
3 tbsp	butter, softened	45 mL
4	bone-in skin-on chicken thighs (about 1 lb/500 g), deboned (see tip, at left)	4
	Salt and ground black pepper	

1. In a medium bowl, toss together apples, sugar and cinnamon. Let stand for 30 minutes. Stir to blend. Stir in carrots, parsley, thyme and sage.

2. In a small bowl, combine garlic and butter. Carefully separate skin from chicken thighs and spread butter mixture evenly under skin.

3. Place a chicken thigh, skin side up, on each prepared foil sheet. Season with salt and pepper. Add apple mixture on top of and around each thigh, dividing evenly. Fold foil into tent-style packets and seal edges tightly.

4. Place packets on hot coals and cook for 20 to 25 minutes, rotating packets a quarter-turn halfway through, until juices run clear when chicken is pierced.

Easy Hawaiian Chicken Dinner

This Hawaiian dinner is often called "haystacks" because the rice forms the base and all the other ingredients get piled on top. It's easy to prepare and easy to alter toppings for different tastes.

Tips

You can substitute cream of chicken soup for the cream of celery.

Shredded rotisserie chicken is an easy substitute for the chicken strips. A 2-lb (1 kg) rotisserie chicken yields about 4 cups (1 L) of white and dark meat. Use about 1 cup (250 mL) per person.

- Prepare campfire coals
- 4 sheets heavy-duty foil, sprayed with nonstick cooking spray

2 cups	cooked long-grain white rice	500 mL
1 cup	ready-to-use chicken broth	250 mL
1	can (10 oz/284 mL) condensed cream of celery soup	1
1 lb	boneless skinless chicken breasts, cut into strips and cooked	500 g
1	red bell pepper, sliced	1
1	onion, sliced	1
1	can (14 oz/398 mL) chopped pineapple, drained	1
1	can (14 oz/398 mL) sliced water chestnuts	1
1	container (5 oz/142 g) chow mein noodles	1

1. In a small bowl, combine rice, bouillon and soup. Let stand for 5 minutes.

2. Divide rice mixture evenly among prepared foil sheets. Top with chicken, red pepper, onion, pineapple and water chestnuts, dividing evenly. Fold foil into tent-style packets and seal edges tightly.

3. Place packets on hot coals and cook for 15 minutes or until vegetables are cooked to desired tenderness. Serve topped with chow mein noodles.

Mandarin Orange Chicken and Broccoli

This is one of my all-time favorite choices for takeout Chinese food. This version is simple enough to take camping and grill over hot coals.

Tips

Prepare the peppers, onions and broccoli at home and pack them in your cooler. They can all be combined in a plastic food storage bag.

Mandarin orange fruit cups come in 4- or 6-count packages. The remaining cups make a great snack or breakfast side.

- Prepare campfire coals
- 6 sheets heavy-duty foil, sprayed with nonstick cooking spray

1½ lbs	boneless skinless chicken (dark or light meat), sliced	750 g
3 cups	cooked rice	750 mL
1	red bell pepper, sliced	1
1	green bell pepper, sliced	1
1	onion, sliced	1
3 cups	broccoli florets	750 mL
2	mandarin orange fruit cups, with juice	2
1 cup	thawed frozen peas	250 mL
3 tbsp	teriyaki sauce	45 mL

1. Divide chicken evenly among prepared foil sheets. Top with rice, red pepper, green pepper, onion, broccoli, oranges and peas, dividing evenly. Drizzle with teriyaki sauce. Fold foil into tent-style packets and seal edges tightly.

2. Place packets on hot coals and cook for 30 minutes, turning packets over occasionally, until vegetables are tender and chicken is no longer pink.

Peach and Ginger–Glazed Pork Chops

Makes 4 servings

These grilled pork chops are infused with flavor from the pairing of peach jam and ginger.

Tip

Serve with a side of Cheesy Chive Green Beans (page 59) for a complete and comforting meal.

- Prepare campfire coals
- 4 double sheets heavy-duty foil, top sheets sprayed with nonstick cooking spray

4	boneless pork chops (about ½ inch/1 cm thick) Salt and ground black pepper	4
2	firm tart apples (such as Granny Smith or Honeycrisp), peeled and sliced	2
1	jar (10 oz/284 mL) peach jam or marmalade	1
1 tsp	grated gingerroot	5 mL
⅓ cup	smooth mustard	75 mL

1. Snip corners of pork chops with a knife or scissors to avoid curling. Place a pork chop on each prepared foil sheet. Season with salt and pepper. Add apples around each pork chop, dividing evenly.

2. In a small bowl, combine jam, ginger and mustard, mixing well. Spoon over top of pork chops. Fold foil into tent-style packets and seal edges tightly.

3. Place packets on hot coals and cook for 15 to 20 minutes, turning packets over halfway through, until just a hint of pink remains in center of pork chop.

Candied Ham and Cranberry Sweet Potatoes

Makes 4 servings

A great combination of flavors comes together in this dish. It will remind you of your favorite holiday at Grandma's house.

Tips

Canned sweet potatoes are often labeled "yams," though they are not, in fact, yams at all.

You can use ½ cup (125 mL) dried cranberries in place of the cranberry sauce. Add enough water (or reserved sweet potato syrup) to cover cranberries in measuring cup.

- Prepare campfire coals
- 4 sheets heavy-duty foil, sprayed with nonstick cooking spray

1	can (15 oz/444 mL) whole sweet potatoes in syrup	1
12 oz	ham, diced (1½ cups/375 mL)	375 g
½ cup	jellied cranberry sauce (about half an 8-oz/228 mL can)	125 mL
3 tbsp	packed brown sugar	45 mL
1 tsp	ground cinnamon	5 mL

1. Drain sweet potatoes, reserving syrup. Cut sweet potatoes into bite-size pieces.

2. Divide ham evenly among prepared foil sheets. Top with sweet potatoes, then with cranberry sauce, dividing evenly. Sprinkle with brown sugar and cinnamon. If desired, drizzle each with up to 1 tbsp (15 mL) reserved sweet potato syrup. Fold foil into tent-style packets and seal edges tightly.

3. Place packets on hot coals and cook for 10 to 15 minutes, turning packets over halfway through, until heated through.

Riverside Ravioli with Ham and Peas

These creamy ravioli packets with ham, cheese and peas are the perfect comfort food for your next camping trip, and they're so easy to make.

Tip

You can choose any type of canned ravioli you like, such as meat-filled or cheese-filled in a meat and tomato sauce.

• Prepare campfire coals, with grate set on top
• 4 sheets heavy-duty foil, sprayed with nonstick cooking spray

12 oz	ham, diced (1½ cups/375 mL)	375 g
1	package (10 oz/300 g) frozen peas, thawed	1
1½ tbsp	Dijon mustard (optional)	22 mL
4	slices Monterey Jack cheese	4
1	can (15 oz/425 g) cheese-filled ravioli in tomato sauce	1
	Grated Parmesan cheese	

1. Divide ham and peas evenly among prepared foil sheets. If using Dijon mustard, spread it on both sides of cheese slices. Place cheese on top of ham and peas. Add ravioli and sauce on top of cheese, dividing evenly. Fold foil into tent-style packets and seal edges tightly.

2. Place packets on grate over hot coals and cook for 20 minutes or until heated through. Serve sprinkled with Parmesan cheese.

Pepperoni Pizza Logs

||||||||||||||||||||||||||||||||||||||||||||||||||||||||||||||||||||||||||||||||||||||||||||||||||||||||||||||||||||||||||||||||||||||||||||||||||||||||||||||||||||||||||||

Makes 4 servings

It doesn't get much easier or more crowd-pleasing than this make-ahead twist on pepperoni pizza.

Tip

If you like to make your own pizza dough, or have a packaged mix you like, you can substitute these for the refrigerated dough. Make sure your dough is not a deep-dish variety.

- 1 double sheet heavy-duty foil, top sheet sprayed with nonstick cooking spray

	All-purpose flour	
1	package (14 oz/398 g) refrigerated pizza dough	1
1	jar (14 oz/398 mL) pizza sauce (1½ cups/375 mL)	1
1½ cups	shredded mozzarella cheese	375 mL
8 oz	thinly sliced pepperoni	250 g
	Dried Italian seasoning (optional)	

Make Ahead

1. On a lightly floured surface, roll pizza dough into a ¼-inch (0.5 cm) thick square.

2. Spread pizza sauce evenly over dough to within ½ inch (1 cm) of edge. Top with cheese and pepperoni. Sprinkle with Italian seasoning (if using). Starting at one end, roll up pizza into a log. Transfer to prepared foil and wrap tightly, sealing all edges. Refrigerate for up to 3 days or freeze for up to 2 months.

At the Campsite

3. Thaw pizza log in cooler if frozen. Meanwhile, prepare campfire coals.

4. Place wrapped pizza log on hot coals and cook for 15 minutes. Turn log over and cook for 10 to 15 minutes or until crust is golden brown and log is heated through. Remove from coals, cut foil open and let rest for 5 minutes before slicing.

Variations

Use 4 oz (125 g) cooked Italian sausage (bulk or casings removed) in place of half of the pepperoni.

Sauté ½ cup (125 mL) thinly sliced onions or green bell peppers (or a combination of both) and add with the pepperoni.

Italian Sausage, Potatoes and Green Beans

Your campers will indeed be happy with this complete Italian-flavored meal in a packet.

Tips

In place of the olive oil, salt and pepper, drizzle your favorite Italian dressing over the other ingredients.

You can use yellow-fleshed potatoes (such as Yukon gold) in place of the red-skinned variety.

- Prepare campfire coals
- 4 sheets heavy-duty foil, sprayed with nonstick cooking spray

8	red-skinned potatoes (about 1 lb/500 g), diced	8
4	Italian sausage links (each about 3 oz/90 g), sliced	4
1 cup	green beans, ends trimmed	250 mL
	Olive oil	
	Salt and ground black pepper	
	Grated Parmesan cheese (optional)	

1. Divide potatoes among prepared foil sheets. Top with sausage and beans, dividing evenly. Drizzle lightly with olive oil. Season with salt and pepper. Fold foil into tent-style packets and seal edges tightly.

2. Place packets on hot coals and cook for 25 to 30 minutes, turning packets over occasionally, until potatoes are soft and sausage is cooked through. Serve sprinkled with Parmesan, if desired.

Bratwurst and Sauerkraut with Grainy Mustard

The smell of bratwurst cooking over an open fire is a classic summertime experience, and the flavor of these bratwurst makes that experience even more delightful.

Tip

If you would like your buns toasted, split them in half and place, cut side down, on grate for 2 to 3 minutes.

- Prepare campfire coals, with grate set on top
- 5 sheets heavy-duty foil, sprayed with nonstick cooking spray

5	bratwurst sausages (each about 3 oz/90 g)	5
1	can (14 oz/398 mL) sauerkraut	1
1 cup	chopped onion	250 mL
5	bratwurst buns or hoagie rolls (see tip, at left)	5
	Grainy mustard	

1. Place a bratwurst on each prepared foil sheet. Top with sauerkraut and onion, dividing evenly. Wrap foil tightly around bratwurst.

2. Place packets on grate over hot coals and cook for 20 to 25 minutes or until bratwurst are browned and cooked through. Remove from grate, open foil to vent and let stand for 2 minutes.

3. Transfer brats to buns and serve with mustard.

Variation

Use Italian or Polish sausage in place of the bratwurst. If using Italian sausage, add 1 cup (250 mL) sliced green bell pepper with the onion.

Pigs in a Blanket with Green Chiles and Cheese

Makes 8 servings

As a kid I loved to make pigs in a blanket and hold them on a stick over the open coals. Kids will have fun preparing this version too, but won't have to stand near a hot campfire to cook their "piggies."

Tip

Use pepper Jack cheese instead of Monterey Jack to kick up the spice level.

- Prepare campfire coals, with grate set on top
- 8 sheets heavy-duty foil, sprayed with nonstick cooking spray

8	frankfurters	8
1	can (4½ oz/127 mL) diced green chiles	1
4	slices Monterey Jack cheese, each cut into 6 strips	4
1	package (8 oz/250 g) refrigerated crescent rolls	1

1. Cut a lengthwise slit into each frankfurter without cutting all the way through. Stuff green chiles into frankfurters, dividing evenly. Insert 3 strips of cheese in each frankfurter.

2. Separate crescent rolls into 8 triangles. Wrap 1 triangle around each frankfurter. Transfer a wrapped frankfurter to each prepared foil sheet. Fold foil into tent-style packets and seal edges tightly.

3. Place packets on grate over hot coals and cook for 12 to 15 minutes, turning packets over once, until crescent roll wraps are golden brown.

Variation

Stuff each frankfurter with 1½ tbsp (22 mL) salsa in place of the green chiles.

Cheesy Chili-Stuffed Hot Dogs

These ballpark-inspired hot dogs pack a lot of punch and are quick and easy to make. Serve with your favorite condiments and you have a home run.

Tips

There are many varieties of canned chili on the market, ranging from sweet to spicy and with or without added peppers or seasonings. Choose the one your campers enjoy most.

Store any leftover chili in an airtight container in your cooler. Use it as a condiment on burgers or brats, or add it to the Lumberjack Breakfast (page 24).

You can wait to add the hot dog buns until after the frankfurters are hot. Open the packets and carefully slide the frankfurters and toppings into the buns.

- Prepare campfire coals
- 4 sheets heavy-duty foil, sprayed with nonstick cooking spray

4	frankfurters	4
4	hot dog buns	4
1	can (15 oz/425 mL) chili without beans	1
½ cup	shredded Cheddar cheese	125 mL
½ cup	chopped onion	125 mL

1. Cut a lengthwise slit into each frankfurter without cutting all the way through. Place frankfurters in buns and place one hot dog on each prepared foil sheet. Stuff 3 tbsp (45 mL) chili into each frankfurter. Top frankfurters with cheese and onions, dividing evenly. Wrap foil tightly around hot dogs.

2. Place packets on hot coals and cook for 10 to 12 minutes or until frankfurters are heated through and cheese is melted.

All-in-One Hot Dog Packets

These zesty hot dog packets include seasoned vegetables, for one easy-to-make meal.

Tip

The vegetable mixture can be prepared ahead of time and refrigerated for up to 2 days.

- Prepare campfire coals
- 2 sheets heavy-duty foil, sprayed with nonstick cooking spray

8	fingerling potatoes, sliced	8
1	small red onion, thinly sliced	1
1	zucchini, thinly sliced	1
2 tbsp	olive oil	30 mL
2 tsp	salt	10 mL
1 tsp	ground black pepper	5 mL
6	frankfurters	6
2 tsp	hot pepper flakes (optional)	10 mL
6	hot dog buns	6

1. In a large sealable plastic bag, combine potatoes, onion, zucchini, oil, salt and pepper. Seal and shake to coat.

2. Add 3 frankfurters to each foil sheet and top with vegetable mixture, dividing evenly. Sprinkle with hot pepper flakes (if using). Fold foil into tent-style packets and seal edges tightly.

3. Place packets on hot coals and cook for 15 to 20 minutes, turning packets over once halfway through, until vegetables are tender. To serve, transfer frankfurters and vegetables to buns.

Variation

For a zesty flavor twist, use an Italian vinaigrette in place of the olive oil and omit the salt and pepper.

Spicy Beef Pita Pockets

Makes 6 servings

This hearty and mouthwatering Middle Eastern–inspired sandwich adds variety to the traditional camping fare. You will be pleasantly surprised by its depth of flavor.

Tip

Pack the airtight container of beef in your cooler and maintain the temperature at or below 40°F (4°C). Be sure to eat the beef within 3 days of when you cooked it.

• 6 sheets heavy-duty foil, sprayed with nonstick cooking spray

Make Ahead

1 tbsp	ground coriander	15 mL
2 tsp	kosher salt	10 mL
1 tsp	ground black pepper	5 mL
1 tsp	paprika	5 mL
1 tsp	hot pepper flakes (optional)	5 mL
2 tbsp	olive oil	30 mL
1 lb	beef flank or sirloin steak, cut into ½-inch (1 cm) thick strips	500 g

At the Campsite

3	6-inch (15 cm) pitas, cut in half crosswise	3
1	onion, chopped	1
1	tomato, chopped	1
1 tbsp	olive oil	15 mL

Make Ahead

1. In a sealable plastic bag, combine coriander, salt, pepper, paprika, hot pepper flakes and oil. Add beef, seal bag and shake to combine. Let stand for 15 minutes.

2. Heat a medium skillet over medium heat. Add beef and marinade; cook, stirring, for 7 to 9 minutes or until beef is no longer pink inside. Let cool completely, then store in an airtight container in the refrigerator for up to 3 days.

At the Campsite

3. Prepare campfire coals. Stuff pita halves with beef, onion and tomato, dividing evenly. Brush outsides of pitas with oil. Place a stuffed pita on each prepared foil sheet. Fold foil into flat packets and seal edges tightly. Place packets on the hot coals and cook for 12 to 15 minutes, turning packets over once halfway through, until heated through and pita bread is slightly golden.

Easy Campfire Philly Cheesesteak Packets

These delicious sandwiches are an extremely popular favorite from Philadelphia. Now you can enjoy them while camping.

Tips

The onion and pepper can be sliced ahead of time and stored in a sealable plastic bag in the refrigerator for up to 3 days or in the freezer for up to 1 month. Let thaw overnight in the refrigerator or cooler.

The steak can be cut into strips and stored in a sealable plastic bag in the refrigerator for up to 3 days or in the freezer for up to 6 months. Let thaw overnight in the refrigerator or cooler.

If you are storing your food in a cooler, make sure the temperature stays below 40°F (4°C).

- Prepare campfire coals
- 4 sheets heavy-duty foil, sprayed with nonstick cooking spray

1	large onion, sliced	1
1	large green bell pepper, sliced	1
1½ lbs	lean tender boneless beef steak (such as sirloin), cut into ½-inch (1 cm) thick strips	750 g
	Salt and ground black pepper	
4	slices provolone or American cheese	4
4	hoagie or soft Italian rolls	4

1. Divide onion and green pepper slices evenly among prepared foil sheets. Layer steak slices on top, dividing evenly. Season with salt and pepper. Fold foil into tent-style packets and seal edges tightly.

2. Place packets, steak side down, on hot coals. Cook for 10 minutes. Turn packets over and remove from coals. Open packets with caution, allowing steam to escape, and add a cheese slice to each packet. Reseal packets and return to coals, seam side up. Cook for 5 to 10 minutes or until cheese is melted. To serve, slide cheesesteak mixture onto rolls.

Backcountry Grilled Beans and Beef Patties

These all-in-one dinner packets are tasty, hearty and filling — the perfect meal after a day of camping activities.

Tips

One of the things I especially like about these dinner packets is that each camper can adjust the toppings to their taste preferences. When you are assembling the packets, ask each camper how much of the beans, onion and bell pepper (if any) they would like.

You can prepare the patties in advance and assemble the packets campside. Beef patties can be wrapped in plastic wrap, then foil, and refrigerated for up to 2 days before they are cooked.

- Prepare campfire coals, with grate set on top
- 4 sheets heavy-duty foil, sprayed with nonstick cooking spray

1 lb	80/20 (lean) ground beef	500 g
¼ cup	dry bread crumbs	60 mL
¼ cup	barbecue sauce	60 mL
	Ground black pepper	
1	can (14 oz/398 mL) baked beans	1
1	onion, sliced crosswise and separated into rings	1
1	small green bell pepper, thinly sliced	1
	Salt (optional)	

1. In a large bowl, using your hands, combine beef, bread crumbs, barbecue sauce and a pinch of pepper. Form into four ½-inch (1 cm) thick patties.

2. Place a patty on each prepared foil sheet. Top with beans, onion and green pepper. Fold foil into tent-style packets and seal edges tightly.

3. Place packets on grate over hot coals and cook for 20 to 30 minutes or until an instant-read thermometer inserted horizontally into the center of a patty registers 160°F (71°C). If desired, season to taste with salt and pepper before serving.

Variation
Substitute pizza sauce for the barbecue sauce.

Big Bear's Meatball Subs

These meatballs are made ahead of time and stored until you are ready to cook them and make hearty and flavorful subs to feed all of your hungry bears at your campsite or tailgate party.

Tips

Two cups (500 mL) of spaghetti sauce is about two-thirds of a 26-oz (740 mL) jar.

If storing the meatballs in a cooler at your campsite, make sure the temperature stays below 40°F (4°C).

The meatballs can be cooked from frozen in step 3, but add 5 minutes to the cooking time.

- Preheat oven to 400°F (200°C)
- Rimmed baking sheet, lined with foil and sprayed with nonstick cooking spray
- 8 sheets heavy-duty foil, sprayed with nonstick cooking spray

Make Ahead

1 lb	80/20 (lean) ground beef	500 g
1 lb	ground pork	500 g
4	large eggs, beaten	4
2	cloves garlic, minced	2
½ cup	dry bread crumbs	125 mL
¼ cup	dehydrated onion flakes	60 mL
¼ cup	grated Parmesan cheese	60 mL
2 tsp	dried basil	10 mL
1 tsp	dried parsley	5 mL
1 tsp	ground black pepper	5 mL

At the Campsite

8	large crusty rolls, split in half	8
2 cups	spaghetti sauce	500 mL
	Additional grated Parmesan cheese (optional)	

Make Ahead

1. In a large bowl, using your hands, combine beef, pork, eggs, garlic, bread crumbs, onion, Parmesan, basil, parsley and pepper. Form into 1-inch (2.5 cm) balls and place on prepared baking sheet, spacing evenly.

2. Bake in preheated oven for 15 to 20 minutes, turning meatballs over halfway through, until no longer pink inside. Let cool completely, then store in the refrigerator for up to 2 days or in the freezer for up to 4 months.

At the Campsite

3. Prepare campfire coals. Place the bottom half of a roll on each prepared foil sheet. Top each with 2 tbsp (30 mL) spaghetti sauce, then with meatballs, dividing evenly. Top meatballs with another 2 tbsp (30 mL) spaghetti sauce per sub, then cover with top half of roll. Fold foil into tent-style packets and seal edges tightly.

4. Place packets on hot coals and cook for 10 to 15 minutes, turning packets over halfway through, until meatballs are heated through. If desired, before serving, lift top halves of rolls to sprinkle meatballs with Parmesan.

Under the Stars Sweet-and-Sour Meatball Subs

Makes 4 servings

These sweet-and-sour meatballs pack a punch of flavor and are delicious served on crusty rolls.

Tips

You can use store-bought frozen meatballs or try the meatball recipe on page 48.

If storing the meatballs in a cooler at your campsite, make sure the temperature stays below 40°F (4°C).

The meatballs can be cooked from frozen in step 3, but add 5 minutes to the cooking time.

- 4 sheets heavy-duty foil, sprayed with nonstick cooking spray

Make Ahead

1	small onion, diced	1
2 tbsp	packed brown sugar	30 mL
¼ cup	ketchup	60 mL
2 tbsp	apple cider vinegar	30 mL

At the Campsite

4	large crusty rolls, split in half	4
12	frozen fully cooked 1-inch (2.5 cm) meatballs, thawed	12

Make Ahead

1. In a medium saucepan, over medium-low heat, combine onion, brown sugar, ketchup and vinegar. Bring to a simmer, stirring occasionally. Simmer, stirring occasionally, for 3 minutes or until sauce is blended. Let cool completely. Transfer to an airtight container and store in the refrigerator for up to 3 days.

At the Campsite

2. Prepare campfire coals. Place the bottom half of a roll on each prepared foil sheet. Place 3 meatballs on each roll. Pour prepared sweet-and-sour sauce over meatballs, dividing evenly, then cover with top half of roll. Fold foil into tent-style packets and seal edges tightly.

3. Place packets on hot coals and cook for 12 to 15 minutes, turning packets over halfway through, until meatballs are heated through.

Camping Recipes: Lunch and Dinner Mains   **49**

Hobo Ground Beef Dinner

Makes 4 servings

This easy to make, all-in-one dinner is a comfort food dream, and it can be easily adjusted to serve one or a crowd.

Tip

Place a lettuce leaf on the bottom of the packet before adding the remaining ingredients and finish with another lettuce leaf on top. This precaution can prevent your food from burning, but you will not want to eat the lettuce.

- Prepare campfire coals
- 4 sheets heavy-duty foil, sprayed with nonstick cooking spray

1 lb	80/20 (lean) ground beef	500 g
1	onion	1
4	carrots, thinly sliced	4
4	potatoes, sliced	4
	Seasoning salt and ground black pepper	

1. Form beef into four $\frac{1}{2}$-inch (1 cm) thick patties.

2. Cut 4 slices from the onion. If desired, finely chop the remaining onion, or reserve it for another use.

3. Place an onion slice on each prepared foil sheet. Add, in this order, one-eighth of the carrots, one-eighth of the potato slices, 1 beef patty, one-eighth of the potato slices and one-eighth of the carrots. Sprinkle with finely chopped onions, if desired. Season with seasoning salt and pepper. Fold foil into tent-style packets and seal edges tightly.

4. Place packets on hot coals and cook for 20 minutes, turning packets over halfway through, until an instant-read thermometer inserted horizontally into the center of a patty registers 160°F (71°C) and vegetables are tender.

Variation

Replace the beef patty with a thawed prepared veggie patty for a complete vegetarian meal.

Beef-Stuffed Pepper Boats

IIIIIIIIIIIIIIIIIIIIIIIIIIIIIIIIIIIIIIIIIIIIIIIIIIIIIIIIIIIIIIIIIIIIIIIIIIIIIIIIIIIIIIIIIIIIIIIIIIIIIIIIIIIIIIIIIIIIIIIIIIIIIIIIIIIIIIIIIIIIIIIIIIIIIIIIIIIIIIIIIIIIIIIIIIIII

Makes 6 servings

These Italian-seasoned stuffed pepper boats have a zesty, full-flavored taste that is very satisfying.

Tips

If you have a 26-oz (740 mL) jar of spaghetti sauce, you'll need about half for this recipe. You can heat the remaining sauce to drizzle over the tops of the peppers. It also makes a great dipping sauce for the Bushwhackers' Chile Cheese Fries on page 54.

It is not necessary to use a mix of bell pepper colors, but if you are serving these on a platter, the presentation is so inviting.

- 6 sheets heavy-duty foil, sprayed with nonstick cooking spray

2 lbs	80/20 (lean) ground beef	1 kg
	Water	
1½ cups	instant brown rice	375 mL
1	zucchini, chopped	1
2 tsp	dried Italian seasoning	10 mL
1⅔ cups	spaghetti sauce, divided	400 mL
1½ cups	shredded mozzarella cheese, divided	375 mL
3	large bell peppers (1 green, 1 red, 1 yellow), halved lengthwise and cored	3

Make Ahead

1. In a large skillet, over medium-high heat, cook beef, breaking it up with a spoon, for 5 to 6 minutes or until no longer pink. Drain off fat.

2. Meanwhile, in a medium saucepan, bring 1½ cups (375 mL) water to a boil over high heat. Stir in rice. Reduce heat to medium-low, cover and simmer for 5 minutes. Remove from heat and let stand for 5 minutes, then stir in beef, zucchini, Italian seasoning, 1 cup (250 mL) spaghetti sauce and 1 cup (250 mL) cheese.

3. Place a pepper half on each prepared foil sheet. Spoon beef mixture into pepper halves, dividing evenly, and top with the remaining sauce and cheese. Fold edges of foil up into a bowl shape around the pepper. Spoon 1 tbsp (15 mL) water into the bottom of each packet. Fold foil into tent-style packets and seal edges tightly. Refrigerate for up to 3 days.

At the Campsite

4. Prepare campfire coals. Place packets on hot coals and cook for 20 to 25 minutes or until filling is heated through and peppers are tender and the edges are crisp.

Lucky Corned Beef and Cabbage Bundles

This Irish-inspired dish with corned beef comes out deliciously moist and flavorful when foil-wrapped and cooked on your campfire.

Tips

The brown sugar adds sweetness and caramelization, but you can omit it if you prefer.

Shred the carrots at home in advance. Place the shredded carrots in an airtight container and cover with cold water and ice to prevent them from drying out.

- Prepare campfire coals
- 4 sheets heavy-duty foil, sprayed with nonstick cooking spray

1	can (10 oz/284 mL) condensed cream of celery soup	1
½ cup	water	125 mL
1 tbsp	packed brown sugar	15 mL
1 tsp	dry mustard	5 mL
1 tsp	dried thyme	5 mL
1 tsp	salt	5 mL
½ tsp	ground black pepper	2 mL
1	head cabbage (about 2 lbs/1 kg)	1
1	can (12 oz/340 g) corned beef, cut into 4 slices	1
4	carrots, shredded	4
2	small onions, thinly sliced	2

1. In a small bowl, combine soup, water, brown sugar, mustard, thyme, salt and pepper.

2. Tear off 8 large outer leaves from the cabbage. Place 1 leaf on each prepared foil sheet and set the remaining leaves aside. Cut off stem and remove hard inner core of cabbage. Cut the remaining cabbage into long strips.

3. Top each cabbage leaf on foil with 1 slice of corned beef. Top with cabbage strips, carrots and onions, dividing evenly. Pour soup mixture over top, dividing evenly. Cover with the remaining cabbage leaves, one per packet. Fold foil into tent-style packets and seal edges tightly.

4. Place packets on hot coals and cook for 20 to 25 minutes or until vegetables are soft.

Hungry Cubs' Loaded Baby Potatoes

These loaded fingerling potatoes make a gratifying and tasty lunch or an exceptional side dish for any meal.

Tips

You can also use yellow-fleshed or red-skinned potatoes in place of the fingerlings. Use 7 to 9 medium, or about 1 lb (500 g) potatoes.

Omit the bacon for a delicious vegetarian dish.

- Prepare campfire coals
- 4 sheets heavy-duty foil, sprayed with nonstick cooking spray

12	large fingerling potatoes, cut into 1-inch (2.5 cm) pieces	12
8	slices bacon, cooked crisp and chopped	8
¼ cup	butter, cut into small pieces	60 mL
2 tsp	seasoning salt	10 mL
1 cup	shredded Cheddar cheese	250 mL
½ cup	chopped green onions	125 mL
	Salt and ground black pepper	
½ cup	sour cream (optional)	125 mL

1. Divide potatoes, bacon and butter evenly among prepared foil sheets. Sprinkle with seasoning salt. Fold foil into tent-style packets and seal edges tightly.

2. Place packets on hot coals and cook for 20 to 25 minutes, turning packets over often, until potatoes are tender. Open packets with caution, allowing steam to escape, and top with cheese and green onions, dividing evenly. Season to taste with salt and pepper. Serve with sour cream on the side, if desired.

Variation

Add ½ cup (125 mL) chopped zucchini or yellow summer squash with the potatoes.

Bushwhackers' Chile Cheese Fries

||||||||||||||||||||||||||||||||||||||||||||||||||||||||||||||||||||||||||||||||||||||||||||||||||||||||||||||||||||||||

Makes 4 servings

These spicy and ooey-gooey fries make the perfect side dish or afternoon or late-night snack. Campers can jump right in and share them.

Tips

When placing the top foil sheet over the fries, make sure it does not touch the cheese.

To see if they are done, check the fries intermittently by opening up a slight fold on the side of the packet.

- Prepare campfire coals, with grate set on top
- 5 sheets heavy-duty foil, 2 sprayed with nonstick cooking spray

1	package (16 oz/500 g) frozen french fries	1
2	cans (each 4½ oz/127 mL) diced green chiles	2
1 cup	shredded Cheddar cheese	250 mL

1. Stack 4 foil sheets, finishing with a sprayed one on top. Spread french fries in the center of the sheets. Top with chiles and cheese, dividing evenly. Tent the remaining sheet of sprayed foil, sprayed side down, over the ingredients. Fold and pinch edges of foil tightly.

2. Place packet on grate over hot coals and cook for 10 to 15 minutes or until fries are cooked to your liking and cheese is melted.

Classic Lyonnaise Potatoes

Simple, quick and
wonderfully tasty, this
is the perfect side dish
to any meal.

Tip
Use 4 prewrapped butter
packets; each packet has the
amount needed per serving.
Keep packets in the cooler,
at or below 40°C (4°F).

• Prepare campfire coals
• 4 sheets heavy-duty foil, sprayed with nonstick cooking spray

4	large russet potatoes, thinly sliced crosswise	4
4	small onions, thinly sliced	4
4 tsp	butter	20 mL
	Salt and ground black pepper	

1. Divide potatoes and onions evenly among prepared foil sheets. Top each with 1 tsp (5 mL) butter and season with salt and pepper. Fold foil into tent-style packets and seal edges tightly.

2. Place packets on hot coals and cook for 15 minutes, turning packets over halfway through, until potatoes are tender.

Peppery Zucchini and Potato Foil Packets

Makes 4 servings

The combination of zucchini, potatoes, peppers and garlic infuses this dish with so much flavor. Your campers will love it.

Tips

For a side dish with Italian flavor, use Italian-seasoned bread crumbs and omit the paprika.

You can prepare the vegetable combination ahead of time and store it in the plastic bag in the refrigerator or cooler for up to 24 hours.

- Prepare campfire coals
- 4 sheets heavy-duty foil, sprayed with nonstick cooking spray

4	russet potatoes, cut into 2-inch (5 cm) cubes	4
2	zucchini, cut into large chunks	2
1	red bell pepper, chopped	1
1	clove garlic, chopped	1
½ cup	dry bread crumbs	125 mL
2 tsp	paprika	10 mL
¼ cup	olive oil	60 mL
	Salt and ground black pepper	

1. In a large sealable plastic bag, combine potatoes, zucchini, red pepper, garlic, bread crumbs, paprika and oil. Season with salt and pepper. Seal bag and shake to coat.

2. Divide potato mixture evenly among prepared foil sheets. Fold foil into tent-style packet and seal edges tightly.

3. Place packets on hot coals and cook for 25 minutes, turning packets over halfway through. Carefully open tops of packets and cook for 5 minutes or until potatoes are tender and bread crumbs are crispy.

Campfire Brown Butter Squash

Makes 4 servings

This squash comes off the campfire tender, sweet and bursting with flavor. It's perfect as a filling side dish to pork, beef or chicken.

Tip

Hot pepper flakes and dried rosemary or thyme are nice substitutions for the cinnamon and nutmeg.

- Prepare campfire coals
- 4 sheets heavy-duty foil, sprayed with nonstick cooking spray

2	small butternut squash, halved lengthwise and seeds removed	2
¼ cup	butter	60 mL
1	onion, chopped	1
2 tbsp	packed brown sugar	30 mL
2 tsp	ground cinnamon	10 mL
1 tsp	ground nutmeg	5 mL
	Salt and ground black pepper	

1. Place a squash half, cut side up, on each prepared foil sheet. Pack butter, onion, sugar, cinnamon and nutmeg into each squash hollow, dividing evenly. Season with salt and pepper. Fold foil into tent-style packets and seal edges tightly.

2. Place packets, cut side up, on hot coals and cook for 40 minutes or until squash is tender.

Rosemary Parmesan Corn on the Cob

Makes 4 servings

Once it occurred to me to season my corn on the cob with Parmesan, it became my first choice of seasonings. I'm confident you will enjoy it as much.

Tips

Transfer the corn packet to the coals carefully and check to make sure you haven't poked any holes or made any tears in the foil.

Hot pepper flakes, to taste, make a nice addition if you like a little bit of spice.

- Prepare campfire coals
- 1 double sheet heavy-duty foil, top sheet sprayed with nonstick cooking spray

4	ears corn, shucked	4
¼ cup	butter, softened	60 mL
	Grated Parmesan cheese	
1 tsp	dried rosemary	5 mL
	Salt and ground black pepper	
4	ice cubes	4

1. Place corn near the center of the prepared foil sheet. Spread butter evenly over corn. Sprinkle with Parmesan and rosemary. Season with salt and pepper. Place ice cubes on top. Fold foil into a tent-style packet and seal edges tightly.

2. Place packet on hot coals and cook for 20 minutes or until corn is tender.

Cheesy Chive Green Beans

Makes 4 servings

So simple, yet so delicious, these browned and crispy green beans are perfect for a quick pick-me-up snack or an easy side dish to grilled burgers, steaks and chicken.

Tips

The Parmesan will turn dark brown, almost black, but don't worry — this gives the beans a nice crunchy texture and wonderful flavor.

If you would like the beans less browned, but still crispy, reduce the cooking time to 15 to 18 minutes.

For more tender green beans, add 3 tbsp (45 mL) water to the bottom of each packet.

- Prepare campfire coals
- 4 sheets heavy-duty foil, sprayed with nonstick cooking spray

1½ lbs	green beans, cut into 2-inch (5 cm) pieces (about 4 cups/1 L)	750 g
½ cup	grated Parmesan cheese	125 mL
2 tsp	chopped fresh chives	10 mL
	Salt and ground black pepper	

1. Divide green beans evenly among prepared foil sheets. Sprinkle with Parmesan and chives. Season with salt and pepper. Fold foil into tent-style packets and seal edges tightly.

2. Place packets on hot coals and cook for 25 to 30 minutes, turning packets over halfway through, until beans are browned and crispy.

Scrumptious Chocolate Cake in Orange Cups

||||||||||||||||||||||||||||||||||||||||||||||||||||||||||||||||||||||||||||||||||||||||||||||||||||||||||||||||||||||||||||||||

Makes 12 servings

Kids of all ages love to experiment, and what better way than baking scrumptious cake in orange shells on the campfire. This recipe is so easy and the potential variations are just about endless.

Tips

Use a fruit-flavored beverage, such as grape, orange or lemon-lime. For a lighter version, try flavored carbonated water.

Leftover orange cups can be individually wrapped tightly in plastic wrap and stored in a cool place for up to 3 days, so your campers can snack on them whenever they like.

- Prepare campfire coals
- 12 sheets heavy-duty foil, sprayed with nonstick cooking spray

12	oranges	12
1	box (16.25 oz/461 g) moist chocolate cake mix	1
1	can or bottle (12 oz/375 mL) fruit-flavored carbonated beverage (see tip, at left)	1

1. Using the palm of your hand, roll oranges on a hard surface to loosen pith from shell. Cut the top third off the oranges. Using a spoon or a small serrated knife, remove insides from both top and bottom sections. (Your campers can eat the orange flesh while waiting for the cakes to bake, or you can reserve the orange flesh to top salads.)

2. In a large sealable plastic bag, prepare cake mix according to package directions, substituting carbonated beverage for any eggs or oil called for. Seal bag and shake to combine. Pour batter into bottom sections of the orange shells, dividing evenly and filling about half full. Place top sections of orange shells on top.

3. Wrap a sheet of foil tightly around each orange shell, leaving a 1-inch (2.5 cm) air pocket on top.

4. Place packets in a stable, upright position on hot coals and cook for 10 to 15 minutes or until a toothpick inserted into the center of a cake comes out clean.

Variations

Tangy Lemon Cake in Orange Cups: Use lemon cake mix and lemon-lime soda.

Ginger Spice Cake in Orange Cups: Use spice cake mix and ginger ale.

Orange Cream Cake in Orange Cups: Use French vanilla cake mix and orange soda.

Cherry and White Chocolate Pound Cakes

Layered cherry and white chocolate cake makes for a really decadent camping dessert. It's so rich and flavorful, you may want to make it at home.

Tips

You should be able to see some of the pie filling between the chocolate chips. If you add too many chips, they will not soften properly.

To make this recipe at home, preheat the oven to 350°F (180°C). Place packets on a rimmed baking sheet and bake for 12 to 15 minutes, turning packets over once, until warmed through and chocolate chips are softened.

A 10-oz (300 g) bag of white chocolate chips will yield about 19 tbsp (285 mL). Save the remaining chips for other recipes.

- Prepare campfire coals, with grate set on top
- 6 sheets heavy-duty foil, sprayed with nonstick cooking spray

1	sheet pound cake (about 13- by 9-inches/33 by 23 cm), cut into 12 even servings	1
1	can (14 oz/398 mL) cherry pie filling	1
6 tbsp	white chocolate chips	90 mL

1. Place a piece of pound cake on each prepared foil sheet. Top with pie filling, dividing evenly, and sprinkle with chocolate chips. Top each with another piece of pound cake. Fold foil into flat packets and seal edges tightly.

2. Place packets on grate over hot coals and cook for 8 to 10 minutes, turning packets over once, until cake is warmed through and chocolate chips are softened.

Pineapple Upside-Down Cakes

This classic dessert is converted here to individual servings that can be cooked over hot coals. The tasty result is sweet, tangy and gooey miniature cakes.

Tips

A 20-oz (625 g) can contains about 10 pineapple rings. Transfer the remaining 4 slices and the juice to an airtight container and refrigerate for up to 3 days. Use in another recipe, such as Tropical Pineapple Donut Bundles (page 18).

- Prepare campfire coals
- 6 sheets heavy-duty foil, sprayed with nonstick cooking spray

½ cup	packed light brown sugar	125 mL
6 tbsp	butter	90 mL
6	pineapple rings	6
6	maraschino cherries, stemmed	6
6	shortcake dessert shells	6

1. To each prepared foil sheet, add 1½ tbsp (22 mL) brown sugar, 1 tbsp (15 mL) butter and 1 pineapple ring. Place a cherry in the middle of each pineapple ring. Place shortcake upside down on top of pineapple. Fold foil into flat packets and seal edges tightly.

2. Place packets, sugar side down, on hot coals and cook for 15 minutes or until pineapple is caramelized. Open packets and turn cakes upside down onto plates.

Campfire Marmalade Waffles

These crispy waffles filled with peach marmalade taste like your favorite peach pie, but are so much easier to make.

Tip

Any type of fruit marmalade will work well in place of peach marmalade in this recipe. Apricot, orange and kumquat are some of my favorites for these waffles.

- Prepare campfire coals, with grate set on top
- 4 sheets heavy-duty foil, sprayed with nonstick cooking spray

8	frozen waffles (any shape)	8
1 cup	peach marmalade	250 mL
	Pancake syrup (optional)	

1. Place 1 waffle on each prepared foil sheet and spread with marmalade. Top each with another waffle. Fold foil into flat packets and seal edges tightly.

2. Place packets on hot coals and cook for 10 to 12 minutes, turning packets over halfway through, until waffles are heated through. Serve with syrup, if desired.

Harvest Apple Crisp

Makes 4 servings

This classic dessert can be made right at your campsite. Make it even more fun by picking up fresh apples at a roadside farmer's stand along the way.

Tips

Premeasure the dry ingredients for the apples and the dry ingredients for the topping ahead of your camping trip. Store in two sealable plastic bags until ready to prepare apple crisp.

The butter can be dropped in small bits on top of the crumb topping if you don't want to cut it in at your campsite.

- Prepare campfire coals, with grate set on top
- 2 double sheets heavy-duty foil, top sheets sprayed with nonstick cooking spray

8 cups	thinly sliced apples (about 2 lbs/1 kg, 6 to 8 apples)	2 L
1 cup	granulated sugar	250 mL
2 tbsp	all-purpose flour	30 mL
1 tsp	ground cinnamon	5 mL
Crumb Topping		
¾ cup	large-flake (old-fashioned) rolled oats	175 mL
½ cup	packed brown sugar	125 mL
½ tsp	salt	2 mL
½ cup	butter, cut into small pieces	125 mL

1. In a large bowl, combine apples, sugar, flour and cinnamon.

2. *Topping:* In a medium bowl, combine oats, brown sugar and salt. Cut in butter.

3. Divide apple mixture evenly between prepared foil sheets. Sprinkle with topping, dividing evenly. Fold foil into flat packets and seal edges tightly.

4. Place packets on grate over hot coals and cook for 20 to 25 minutes, rotating packets occasionally for even heat, until apples are tender. Open packets and divide into 4 servings.

Raspberry Bread Pudding

This bread pudding is crispy on the outside, with creamy raspberry-soaked bread on the inside. Overall, it's a delectable way to finish any meal.

Tips

Whole or 2% milk works best in this recipe. Lower-fat milk can make the pudding more runny and less rich. However, use whatever you have on hand at your campsite.

You can use breads other than sourdough, but they should be similar in texture. Challah is a nice alternative; just note that it will make the pudding a bit sweeter.

If you use fresh raspberries in this recipe and are bringing them from home, plan to make this dessert within 2 to 3 days after purchasing your berries. If you are lucky enough to pick fresh raspberries while camping, rinse them carefully and check for any small bugs hiding in them.

- Prepare campfire coals, with grate set on top
- 4 sheets heavy-duty foil, sprayed with nonstick cooking spray

1 cup	granulated sugar	250 mL
2 tsp	ground cinnamon	10 mL
4	large eggs	4
2 cups	milk (see tip, at left)	500 mL
1 tsp	vanilla extract	5 mL
8 cups	sourdough bread cubes (about a 2-lb/1 kg loaf)	2 L
2 cups	thawed frozen or fresh raspberries	500 mL

1. In a large bowl, whisk together sugar, cinnamon, eggs, milk and vanilla. Fold in bread cubes and berries. Let stand for 30 minutes.

2. Divide pudding evenly among prepared foil sheets. Fold foil into flat packets and seal edges tightly.

3. Place packets on grate over hot coals and cook for 35 minutes, turning packets over three or four times, until mixture has gelled together.

Stuffed Banana Boats

||||||||||||||||||||||||||||||||||||||||||||||||||||||||||||||||||||||||||||||||||||||||||||||||||||||||||||||||||||||||

Makes 4 servings

Similar to a banana split but without the ice cream, these banana boats are just as delicious and are so fun to make again and again with a variety of fillings.

Tips

A 16-oz (500 g) bag of mini marshmallows will yield about 10 cups (2.5 L). Use what you need for this recipe and save the rest to make Marshmallow Butterscotch Cones (page 70).

A 10-oz (300 g) bag of chocolate chips will yield about 19 tbsp (285 mL). Save the remainder for another dessert, or substitute butter-scotch chips in this recipe and use the remainder for the Marshmallow Butterscotch Cones.

- Prepare campfire coals
- 4 sheets heavy-duty foil, sprayed with nonstick cooking spray

4	large ripe bananas (peel intact)	4
2 cups	mini marshmallows	500 mL
4 tbsp	chocolate chips	60 mL

1. Peel back one section of each banana, leaving peel attached. Cut a small groove down the length of the banana. Pack marshmallows and chocolate chips into the groove. Replace banana peel over the fillings. Wrap each banana tightly in foil.

2. Place packets on hot coals and cook for 5 minutes or until chocolate is melted. Peel back the same section of peel and eat the banana right out of the peel.

Variation

For a supersized banana split version, add strawberry jam, crushed pineapple and chopped nuts on top of the marshmallows and chocolate chips.

Glazed Fruity Banana Slices

||||||||||||||||||||||||||||||||||||||||||||||||||||||||||||||||||||||||||||||||||||||||||||||||||||||||||||||||||||||||||||||

These delightfully sweet and creamy banana slices are a scrumpdillyicious treat. After all, what hardy camper wouldn't love gooey bananas with a sweet and fruity topping?

Tips

Serve the bananas over ice cream, sugar cookies, graham crackers or pound cake.

Apricot or apple jam work equally well in this recipe in place of the peach jam.

- Prepare campfire coals, with grate set on top
- Double extra-large sheet heavy-duty foil, top sheet sprayed with nonstick cooking spray

¼ cup	packed dark brown sugar	60 mL
¼ cup	pineapple or orange juice	60 mL
3 tbsp	peach jam	45 mL
2 tbsp	butter, softened	30 mL
2 tbsp	lemon juice	30 mL
4	large ripe bananas, cut into 1-inch (2.5 cm) slices	4

1. In a medium bowl, combine brown sugar, pineapple juice, jam, butter and lemon juice.

2. Arrange bananas in center of prepared foil sheet, without overlapping. Fold edges of foil up into a bowl shape around bananas. Pour and spread jam mixture over bananas. Fold foil into a tent-style packet and seal edges tightly.

3. Place packet on grate over hot coals and cook for 10 to 15 minutes or until bananas are softened and evenly coated. Carefully open packet and cook for 3 to 5 minutes or until bananas are glazed to your liking. Using a large spoon, carefully transfer individual servings to plates.

Salted Caramel Pears

Sweet, creamy and juicy pears get special treatment with a simple salted caramel topping. The result is sweet, sour and salty flavors bundled into one little package.

Tip

If you can't find Anjou pears, choose a variety that is similar in shape: large and with a short neck.

- Prepare campfire coals, with grate set on top
- 4 sheets heavy-duty foil, sprayed with nonstick cooking spray

¼ cup	packed brown sugar	60 mL
¼ cup	butter, softened	60 mL
2	red or green Anjou pears (see tip, at left), cut in half lengthwise and cored	2
½ cup	orange juice	125 mL
	Coarse salt	

1. In a small bowl, combine brown sugar and butter.

2. Place a pear half, cored side up, on each prepared foil sheet. Pack butter mixture into the pear hollows, dividing evenly. Drizzle orange juice over top. Sprinkle with salt. Fold foil into tent-style packets and seal edges tightly.

3. Place packets on grate over hot coals and cook for 45 minutes, moving packets often, until pears are caramelized.

Cinnamon Orange Slice Goodies

These orange slices come off the campfire sweet, tangy and caramelized. Serve them for dessert or as a sweet, tasty snack anytime.

Tip

You can use reserved pineapple juice from other recipes in this chapter or buy a small can or drink box of pineapple juice.

- Prepare campfire coals
- 4 sheets heavy-duty foil, sprayed with nonstick cooking spray

4	seedless oranges, peeled and separated into sections	4
2 tbsp	packed brown sugar	30 mL
½ tsp	ground cinnamon	2 mL
⅓ cup	pineapple or apple juice	75 mL
2 tbsp	butter	30 mL

1. Divide orange sections evenly among prepared foil sheets. Sprinkle with brown sugar and cinnamon. Fold edges of foil up into a bowl shape around the oranges. Pour pineapple juice over top and dot with butter. Fold foil into flat packets and seal edges tightly.

2. Place packets on hot coals and cook for 20 to 22 minutes or until oranges are hot and caramelized.

Variation

For a more decadent, adult version of this recipe, substitute rum for the pineapple juice.

Marshmallow Butterscotch Cones

Makes 12 servings

This is one dessert your campers will ask for again and again. The variations are almost endless, to please just about anyone.

Tips

In place of the English toffee bits, you can use four 1.4-oz (38 g) chocolate-covered toffee bars, chopped. You can also use plain toffee bars (without the chocolate), chopped.

You can make as many or as few cones as you want, but the ice cream cones tend to come in 12-count containers.

Do not overfill your cones or they will not melt properly. Your campers can snack on any leftover toppings or use them in other recipes.

Use leftover marshmallows and butterscotch chips to make the Stuffed Banana Boats (page 66).

- Prepare campfire coals
- 12 sheets heavy-duty foil, sprayed with nonstick cooking spray

12	sugar ice cream cones	12
1	bag (16 oz/500 g) mini marshmallows	1
1	bag (10 oz/300 g) butterscotch chips	1
1	bag (8 oz/250 g) English toffee bits (see tip, at left)	1
	Sprinkles (optional)	

1. In each cone, layer marshmallows, butterscotch chips and toffee bits as many times as needed until cone is full. Wrap cones tightly in prepared foil sheets.

2. Stick cones upright in hot coals and cook for 5 minutes or until ingredients are melted. Remove from coals and let cool slightly before opening. Top with sprinkles, if desired.

Variation

Replace the butterscotch chips and/or the toffee bits with dark, semisweet or white chocolate chips, peanut butter chips, chopped nuts, shredded coconut, dried fruit, caramel squares or bits, or candy bars cut into chunks. Keep in mind that the cones must always contain marshmallows for the ingredients to meld.

No Fail S'mores

If you have ever carefully toasted a marshmallow over a campfire only to watch it go spinning off and down into the coals, you will appreciate the simplicity and marshmallow-saving joy of this recipe.

Tip
Open packets carefully to avoid burns from the melted marshmallows and chocolate.

- Prepare campfire coals
- 4 sheets heavy-duty foil, sprayed with nonstick cooking spray

4	graham crackers (about 3 inches/ 7.5 cm square)	4
2	milk chocolate bars (each 1½ oz/43 g), broken in half	2
4	large marshmallows	4

1. Place 1 graham cracker half on each prepared foil sheet. Top each with 1 chocolate bar half and 1 marshmallow. Place another graham cracker half on top and press lightly together. Fold foil into flat packets and seal edges tightly.

2. Place packets on hot coals and cook for 4 to 5 minutes, turning packets over once, until marshmallows are melted.

Variation
Use dark chocolate bars, bars with nuts or cookies 'n' crème bars in place of the milk chocolate bars.

Grilling Recipes

Tailgaters' Coconut Shrimp Dip

This scrumptious dip will remind you of your favorite coconut shrimp appetizer, but with no deep-frying required. Easy to make, store and transport, it is the ideal tailgating appetizer.

Tips

To toast coconut, preheat oven to 350°F (180°C). Spread coconut on a baking sheet and bake for 5 to 7 minutes, stirring occasionally, until light golden brown. Check on the coconut often, to prevent burning.

If you are storing and transporting your dip, after step 1 refrigerate the wrapped dish or store it in a cooler at or below 40°F (4°C). Increase the grilling time to 15 to 18 minutes.

- Preheat barbecue grill to medium heat
- 9-inch (23 cm) disposable foil pie plate, sprayed with nonstick cooking spray
- Large sheet heavy-duty foil

8 oz	cream cheese, softened	250 g
1 cup	shredded mozzarella cheese	250 mL
Pinch	dried mint	Pinch
	Grated zest and juice of ½ lime	
4 oz	cooked shrimp, chopped	125 g
¼ cup	sweetened flaked coconut, toasted (see tip, at left)	60 mL
1	box (13.7 oz/388 g) round snack crackers (such as Ritz), divided	1

1. In a medium bowl, combine cream cheese, mozzarella, mint, lime zest and lime juice until well blended. Spread mixture in bottom of prepared pie plate. Sprinkle evenly with shrimp and coconut. Crush 6 crackers and sprinkle over top. Wrap plate in foil and seal edges tightly.

2. Place wrapped plate on preheated grill and cook for 12 to 14 minutes or until hot and bubbly. Remove from grill and let stand for 5 minutes. Serve dip with the remaining crackers.

Variation

Use a pinch of dried basil, marjoram or rosemary in place of the mint.

Jalapeño Popper Starters

Get a little fire raging in your belly before the game with these cheese-stuffed jalapeño poppers. They are perfect for tailgating or serving at home during the game.

Tips

Always use kitchen gloves when handling jalapeños to avoid irritating and burning your skin. Avoid touching your eyes after touching jalapeños.

A small melon baller works very well for scooping out the center of the jalapeños.

Gruyère and Emmental cheese melt very well and are a nice substitute for the cream cheese. Shred either type with a box grater or rasp grater, such as a Microplane, before adding to the bowl. You will need 2 cups (500 mL) shredded (about an 8-oz/250 g block of cheese).

Jalapeño packets can be prepared through step 3 and refrigerated or stored in a cooler at or below 40°F (4°C). Increase the grilling time to 12 to 15 minutes for cold packets.

- Preheat barbecue grill to medium-high heat
- Pastry bag fitted with a large round tip
- 8 sheets heavy-duty foil, cut in half, sprayed with nonstick cooking spray

1 lb	cream cheese, softened	500 g
2 tbsp	freshly squeezed lime juice	30 mL
½ tsp	garlic powder	2 mL
½ tsp	onion powder	2 mL
½ tsp	sweet smoked paprika	2 mL
16	medium jalapeño peppers, stem removed, seeds and pith scooped out (see tips, at left)	16

1. In a medium bowl, combine cream cheese, lime juice, garlic powder, onion powder and paprika.

2. Fill pastry bag with cream cheese mixture. Pipe cream cheese mixture into each jalapeño, dividing evenly.

3. Place a filled jalapeño on each prepared foil sheet half. Wrap foil tightly around jalapeño, making a tent-style seal over the filling.

4. Place wrapped jalapeños on preheated grill and cook for 10 minutes, turning packets over often, until cheese is melted.

Jamaican Jerk Chicken Wings

Makes 6 to 12 servings

This chicken wings recipe has a fiery taste with a bit of sweet and sour mixed in to get those taste buds jumping.

Tips

If this is the only appetizer or one of a few appetizers you will be serving, allow for 6 wing sections per person. If you are serving more appetizers or snacks, allow for 3 wing sections per person.

If you can find presplit wings, you'll save time because you won't have to cut and separate the wing sections.

- 6 double sheets heavy-duty foil, top sheets sprayed with nonstick cooking spray

2/3 cup	Jamaican jerk sauce	150 mL
2 tbsp	packed brown sugar	30 mL
1 tbsp	kosher salt	15 mL
3 tbsp	vegetable oil	45 mL
2 tbsp	freshly squeezed lime juice	30 mL
18	chicken wings, sections split apart, wing tips reserved or discarded	18
2/3 cup	chopped green onions	150 mL

1. In a large sealable plastic bag, combine jerk sauce, brown sugar, salt, oil and lime juice. Add wings, seal and shake to coat. Let marinate in the refrigerator for at least 1 hour or up to 2 hours before grilling.

2. Preheat barbecue grill to high heat.

3. Transfer 6 wing sections to center of each prepared foil sheet. Fold edges of foil up into a box shape around the wings. Drizzle the remaining marinade evenly over wings. Fold foil into flat packets and seal edges tightly.

4. Place packets on grill and cook for 25 minutes, turning packets over once, until juices run clear when chicken is pierced. Serve sprinkled with green onions.

Tex-Mex Chicken and Corn Quesadillas

These fun and flavorful quesadillas are great for a quick lunch or perfect as game-day appetizers.

Tips

You can substitute ¾ cup (175 mL) thawed frozen corn for the canned corn.

Serve with sour cream and guacamole on the side.

If you are serving this as an appetizer, with other appetizers, it will serve about 8.

• Preheat barbecue grill to medium heat
• 4 sheets heavy-duty foil, sprayed with nonstick cooking spray

8	8-inch (20 cm) flour tortillas	8
1 cup	chopped rotisserie chicken	250 mL
1 cup	shredded pepper Jack cheese	250 mL
1	can (8 oz/227 mL) corn kernels, drained	1
	Chopped fresh cilantro	

1. Place 1 tortilla on each prepared foil sheet. Spread chicken, cheese and corn over top, dividing equally. Season with cilantro. Top each with another tortilla. Fold foil into flat packets and seal edges tightly.

2. Place packets on preheated grill and cook for 5 minutes, turning packets over once, until cheese is melted and quesadillas are heated through. Cut quesadillas into quarters before serving.

Margherita Flatbread Pizza

Makes 4 servings

Melted fresh mozzarella cheese and torn fresh basil are the centerpieces that make this classic pizza an all-time favorite.

Tips

If using rectangular flatbreads, 7- by 5-inch (18 by 13 cm) slices work best.

You can increase the amount of tomato sauce to your taste, but do so in small increments.

You can use prebaked pizza rounds instead of flatbread.

- Preheat barbecue grill to medium-high heat
- 4 sheets heavy-duty foil, sprayed with nonstick cooking spray

4	6-inch (15 cm) round flatbread slices (see tip, at left)	4
1	can (8 oz/227 mL) tomato sauce	1
	Extra virgin olive oil	
6	fresh basil leaves, roughly torn, divided	6
4 oz	fresh mozzarella cheese, cut into ¼-inch (0.5 cm) slices	125 g

1. Place a slice of flatbread on each prepared foil sheet. Using the back of a spoon, spread one-quarter of sauce over each flatbread. Drizzle with oil and sprinkle evenly with half the basil. Arrange mozzarella on top, dividing evenly. Sprinkle the remaining basil evenly over the cheese. Fold foil into tent-style packets and seal edges tightly.

2. Place packets on preheated grill and cook for 6 to 8 minutes, rotating packets a quarter-turn halfway through, until cheese is melted. Check often and remove flatbread from the grill before it starts to char.

Quinoa-Stuffed Bell Peppers

Full of flavor and fiber, these stuffed peppers are a tantalizing, filling main dish or side. The vegetarian version can be easily adapted to satisfy meat eaters (see variation).

Tip

If you are doing a combination of vegetarian and meat-stuffed peppers (see variation), use different colors of bell peppers to distinguish between the two versions.

- Preheat barbecue grill to medium-high heat
- 6 sheets heavy-duty foil, sprayed with nonstick cooking spray

1	small zucchini, chopped	1
2 cups	cooked quinoa	500 mL
2 cups	frozen vegetarian crumbles	500 mL
1½ cups	shredded mozzarella cheese, divided	375 mL
1 tsp	dried Italian seasoning	5 mL
1½ cups	tomato pasta sauce, divided	375 mL
1	large red bell pepper, halved lengthwise and seeded	1
1	large green bell pepper, halved lengthwise and seeded	1
1	large yellow bell pepper, halved lengthwise and seeded	1
6 tbsp	water	90 mL

1. In a large bowl, combine zucchini, quinoa, vegetarian crumbles, 1 cup (250 mL) mozzarella, Italian seasoning and 1 cup (250 mL) pasta sauce.

2. Spoon quinoa mixture into pepper halves, dividing evenly. Place a stuffed pepper on each prepared foil sheet. Top with the remaining pasta sauce and cheese, dividing evenly. Fold edges of foil up into a bowl shape around the peppers. Pour 1 tbsp (15 mL) water into the bottom of each packet. Fold foil into tent-style packets and seal edges tightly.

3. Place packets on preheated grill and cook for 20 to 25 minutes or until filling is heated through and peppers are tender-crisp.

Variations

If preparing this dish for meat eaters, substitute an equal amount of cooked ground beef for the vegetarian crumbles. You'll need to cook about 2½ lbs (1.25 kg) ground beef.

Substitute cooked brown or white rice for the quinoa.

Steaming Flounder Rollups with Horseradish Sauce

Flounder gets special treatment with these decadent little rollups stuffed with spinach and horseradish crème fraîche. Serve with a rice pilaf for a light and gratifying meal.

Tips

Orange roughy or sole fillets can be substituted for the flounder.

If you cannot find crème fraîche, replace it with a mixture of ¼ cup (60 mL) soft cream cheese spread and ¼ cup (60 mL) sour cream.

• Preheat barbecue grill to medium heat
• 4 sheets heavy-duty foil, sprayed with nonstick cooking spray

½ cup	crème fraîche	125 mL
1 tbsp	prepared horseradish	15 mL
½ tsp	kosher salt, divided	2 mL
1 lb	skinless flounder fillet, cut into 4 pieces	500 g
2 cups	packed trimmed spinach leaves	500 mL
	Extra virgin olive oil	
¼ cup	crushed garlic-flavored croutons	60 mL

1. In a small bowl, combine crème fraîche, horseradish and ½ tsp (2 mL) salt.

2. Place a fish fillet on each prepared foil sheet. Spread horseradish crème fraîche on top, dividing evenly. Top with layers of spinach, dividing evenly. Roll up each fish fillet jelly roll–style and position seam side down. Brush with oil and sprinkle with croutons, rolling fillets as needed to coat all sides in croutons. Roll foil around the fish rolls and seal edges tightly.

3. Place packets on preheated grill and cook for 15 minutes, turning packets over once, until crumbs are golden and fish is opaque and flakes easily when tested with a fork. Remove from grill and open packets with caution, allowing steam to escape. Let stand for 5 minutes before serving.

Ginger Soy Salmon with Lemon Caper Butter

||||||||||||||||||||||||||||||||||||||||||||||||||||||||||||||||||||||||||||||||||||||||||||||||||||||||||||||||||||||||||

Makes 6 servings

Deeply flavorful salmon is grilled with ginger, garlic and soy sauce, then drizzled with a decadent buttery lemon caper sauce for pure delight.

Tip

Steelhead or ocean trout is a nice alternative to salmon. It is very similar in flavor, color, texture and omega-3 fat content, but is typically less expensive than salmon.

- Preheat barbecue grill to medium heat
- 6 sheets heavy-duty foil, sprayed with nonstick cooking spray

2 tbsp	soy sauce	30 mL
1 tbsp	unseasoned rice vinegar	15 mL
2 tsp	sesame or sunflower oil	10 mL
6	skin-on salmon fillets (each about 4 oz/125 g)	6
2	cloves garlic, sliced	2
1	1-inch (2.5 cm) piece gingerroot, sliced	1
3 tbsp	chopped fresh parsley	45 mL
¼ cup	drained capers	60 mL
¼ cup	butter	60 mL
	Grated zest and juice of 1 lemon	

1. In a small bowl, whisk together soy sauce, vinegar and oil.

2. Place a fish fillet, skin side down, on each prepared foil sheet. Fold edges of foil up into a bowl shape around the fish. Pour in soy sauce mixture, dividing evenly. Arrange garlic and ginger slices evenly on top of salmon. Fold foil into flat packets and seal edges tightly.

3. Place packets, seam side up, on preheated grill and cook for about 10 minutes or until fish is opaque and flakes easily when tested with a fork.

4. Meanwhile, in a small saucepan over medium heat, combine parsley, capers, butter, lemon zest and lemon juice. Heat, stirring, for 3 to 5 minutes or until butter is melted and mixture is blended.

5. Serve fish drizzled with lemon caper butter.

Grilled Sole and Artichoke Hearts

IIIIIIIIIIIIIIIIIIIIIIIIIIIIIIIIIIIIIIIIIIIIIIIIIIIIIIIIIIIIIIIIIIIIIIIIIIIIIIIIIIIIIIIIIIIIIIIIIIIIIIII

Makes 4 servings

Simple to prepare and clean up, this moist and creamy fillet of sole paired with sweet and tangy artichokes is a meal you will enjoy on many levels.

Tips

Flavored soft cream cheese spreads, such as chive and onion or garden vegetable, would also work nicely in this recipe.

If desired, you can use a low-fat or nonfat cream cheese spread.

- Preheat barbecue grill to medium heat
- 4 sheets heavy-duty foil, sprayed with nonstick cooking spray

2	lemons, thinly sliced	2
8	skinless sole fillets (about 1 lb/500 g total)	8
½ cup	soft cream cheese spread	125 mL
2	green onions, thinly sliced	2
1	jar (2 oz/57 mL) diced pimientos, drained	1
1	can (14 oz/398 mL) artichoke hearts, drained	1
½ cup	freshly grated Parmesan cheese	125 mL

1. Arrange lemon slices in a square, overlapping slightly, on prepared foil sheets, dividing evenly.

2. Spread one side of each fish fillet with cream cheese spread and sprinkle with green onions and pimientos. Starting at the narrow end, roll up fish fillets jelly roll–style. Place 2 fillets per packet, seam side down, on top of lemons. Add artichoke hearts alongside fish, dividing evenly. Sprinkle with Parmesan. Fold foil into tent-style packets and seal edges tightly.

3. Place packets on preheated grill and cook for 10 to 12 minutes or until fish is opaque and flakes easily when tested with a fork.

Tilapia and Asparagus with Creamy Parmesan Sauce

You will love this simple yet elegant dish of moist, flaky tilapia with a delectable Parmesan sauce and asparagus spears.

Tip

Any other lean, flaky white fish, such as flounder, can be used in place of the tilapia.

• Preheat barbecue grill to medium-high heat
• 4 sheets heavy-duty foil, sprayed with nonstick cooking spray

¼ cup	freshly grated Parmesan cheese	60 mL
¼ cup	mayonnaise	60 mL
4	skin-on tilapia fillets (each about 5 oz/150 g)	4
24	spears asparagus (about 1 lb/500 g), trimmed	24
	Kosher salt and freshly ground black pepper	
1 tbsp	drained capers	15 mL
	Lemon wedges (optional)	

1. In a small bowl, combine Parmesan and mayonnaise.

2. Place a fish fillet, skin side down, on each prepared foil sheet. Using a basting brush, spread Parmesan sauce over the top of each fillet, dividing evenly. Arrange 6 asparagus spears around each fillet. Season to taste with salt and pepper. Garnish with capers. Fold foil into tent-style packets and seal edges tightly.

3. Place packets on preheated grill and cook for 10 to 12 minutes or until fish is opaque and flakes easily when tested with a fork. If desired, squeeze juice from lemon wedges over fish before serving.

Basil Pesto Tilapia with Rice Pilaf

Made-from-scratch basil pesto adds the crowning touch to the light and flaky tilapia, which gets a flavorful pick-me-up from savory seasonings and rosemary.

Tips

Snapper, grouper or flounder are nice substitutes for the tilapia, but you can use any firm white fish.

In place of the rice pilaf, you can use a cooked wild rice blend or any rice blend you like.

- Preheat barbecue grill to medium heat
- 6 sheets heavy-duty foil, sprayed with nonstick cooking spray

1 tbsp	paprika	15 mL
1 tsp	garlic powder	5 mL
¼ tsp	kosher salt	1 mL
¼ tsp	freshly ground black pepper	1 mL
¼ tsp	dried rosemary	1 mL
6	skinless tilapia fillets (each about 5 oz/150 g)	6
3 tbsp	virgin olive oil	45 mL
¾ cup	Basil Pesto (see recipe, opposite)	175 mL
3½ cups	cooked rice pilaf	875 mL

1. In a small bowl, combine paprika, garlic powder, salt, pepper and rosemary.

2. Brush both sides of fish fillets with oil and pat with dry rub, coating evenly. Place a fillet on each prepared foil sheet. Top each fillet with 2 tbsp (30 mL) pesto. Arrange rice blend around fish, dividing evenly. Fold foil into flat packets and seal edges tightly.

3. Place packets on preheated grill and cook for 10 to 12 minutes or until fish is opaque and flakes easily when tested with a fork.

**Makes about
1½ cups (375 mL)**

This easy basil pesto can be used in place of a red sauce as a pizza topping, spread on crostini with a slice of fresh mozzarella, mixed into yogurt or sour cream for dips, or blended with buttermilk for a creamy salad dressing. Once you have it in your arsenal, you will want to use it again and again.

Tip

Store pesto in an airtight container in the refrigerator for up to 3 days or in the freezer for up to 1 month. Try freezing it in ice cube trays, then transferring the frozen cubes to freezer bags. One ice cube equals about 1 tbsp (15 mL) pesto.

Basil Pesto

- Small food processor

1 cup	packed fresh basil leaves	250 mL
2	cloves garlic	2
¼ cup	extra virgin olive oil	60 mL
⅓ cup	freshly grated Parmesan cheese	75 mL
¼ cup	pine nuts	60 mL
2 tbsp	freshly squeezed lemon juice	30 mL
	Kosher salt and freshly ground black pepper	

1. In food processor, combine basil and garlic; pulse to combine. Pulsing continuously, gradually add oil through the feed tube. Add Parmesan, pine nuts, lemon juice and salt and pepper to taste; process until pesto is smooth or your desired consistency.

Lemon Dill Rainbow Trout with Carrots and Fennel

Makes 4 servings

You will love the fresh, lively citrus taste of the rainbow trout, paired with orange-glazed carrots and a hint of licorice.

Tip

If transferring to plates to serve, pour the juices from the bottom of foil packets over the fish and vegetables.

- Preheat barbecue grill to medium heat
- 4 sheets heavy-duty foil, sprayed with nonstick cooking spray

4	carrots, julienned	4
1	small bulb fennel (about 8 oz/250 g), julienned	1
3 tbsp	orange juice	45 mL
1 tbsp	virgin olive oil	15 mL
	Kosher salt	
4	rainbow trout fillets (each about 5 oz/150 g)	4
	Freshly ground black pepper	
2 tbsp	butter, thinly sliced	30 mL
1	lemon, thinly sliced	1
4	fresh dill sprigs, chopped	4

1. In a medium bowl, toss together carrots, fennel, orange juice, oil and 1 tsp (5 mL) salt.

2. Lay a fish fillet, skin side down, on each prepared foil sheet. Sprinkle liberally with salt and pepper. Top fish with butter slices, then lemon slices, dividing evenly. Sprinkle with dill. Add vegetable mixture alongside fish, dividing evenly. Fold foil into tent-style packets and seal edges tightly.

3. Place packets on preheated grill and cook for 10 to 12 minutes, rotating packets occasionally, until vegetables are tender and fish is opaque and flakes easily when tested with a fork.

Portuguese Clam Bake with Corn on the Cob

Makes 4 servings

There is nothing quite like the wow factor of opening up a pot of boiled clams, but this easy-to-prepare clam bake delivers the same amazing aroma and flavor as each diner opens their individual packet.

Tips

I used larger sheets of foil in this recipe to accommodate the clams and corn cobs. The square sheets more closely mimic the traditional clambake pots.

Purchase clams from a known and trusted supplier. If buying them in a bag, check for a certification number on the label. Discard any clams that have cracked or broken shells. Before cooking, tap each shell gently — the clam should close when tapped; discard any that do not.

You can substitute dry-cured chorizo or andouille sausage for the linguiça.

- Preheat barbecue grill to medium-high heat
- Four 12-inch (30 cm) square sheets cheesecloth
- Four 24-inch (60 cm) square sheets heavy-duty foil

48	small clams (about 2 lbs/1 kg), scrubbed	48
2 lbs	linguiça sausage, cut into chunks	1 kg
2 lbs	new potatoes (about 24 to 30), quartered	1 kg
4	cloves garlic, sliced	4
2	ears sweet corn, shucked and cut into quarters	2
¼ cup	Old Bay seasoning	60 mL
2	bottles (each 12 oz/341 mL) beer	2
	Virgin olive oil	
1 cup	butter, melted	250 mL
2 tbsp	chopped fresh parsley	30 mL

1. Place a sheet of cheesecloth on top of each foil sheet. Add clams, dividing evenly. Top with sausages, potatoes, garlic and corn, dividing evenly. Sprinkle with Old Bay seasoning. Fold edges of foil up into a bowl shape around the clam mixture and pour ½ bottle of beer into each packet. Drizzle lightly with olive oil. Fold foil into tent-style packets and seal edges tightly.

2. Place packets on preheated grill and cook for 20 to 25 minutes or until potatoes are tender and clams have opened. Remove from grill and open packets with caution, allowing steam to escape. Discard any clams that have not opened. Drizzle clam mixture with melted butter and garnish with parsley.

Sizzling Scallops with Lemon Garlic Asparagus

Makes 4 servings

Wrapping scallops and asparagus in foil is the ideal way to keep them moist and tender while infusing them with incredible flavor.

Tip

If asparagus is not tender-crisp when the scallops are done, remove scallops from packets and keep warm. Continue to cook asparagus in the packets for 3 to 5 minutes, or as needed.

- Preheat barbecue grill to medium heat
- 4 sheets heavy-duty foil, sprayed with nonstick cooking spray

4	sprigs fresh thyme, stems removed	4
3	cloves garlic, minced	3
3 tbsp	virgin olive oil	45 mL
24	spears asparagus, trimmed	24
12 oz	sea scallops (20 to 30 count), side muscles removed	375 g
	Kosher salt	
1 tsp	ground lemon pepper	5 mL
1	lemon, cut into wedges (optional)	1

1. In a small bowl, whisk together thyme leaves, garlic and oil.

2. Divide asparagus spears evenly among prepared foil sheets. Arrange 5 to 7 scallops alongside asparagus spears, creating a long rectangle. Drizzle oil mixture over top. Season liberally with salt and lemon pepper. Fold foil into tent-style packets and seal edges tightly.

3. Place packets on preheated grill and cook for 2 to 3 minutes per side, turning packets over once, until asparagus is tender-crisp (see tip, at left) and scallops are firm and opaque.

Creole Shrimp and Sausage with Red Beans and Rice

Makes 4 servings

Creole cooking is a mélange of flavors inspired by French and Spanish cuisines, as well as the recipes of Louisiana's native inhabitants. This tantalizing Creole dish showcases many of the traditional ingredients.

Tips

If you can only find larger cans of kidney beans, you'll need 1½ cups (375 mL) drained beans for this recipe.

Adjust the amount of Creole seasoning as desired, keeping in mind that the flavor will become more intense during cooking.

- Preheat barbecue grill to medium-low heat
- 4 sheets heavy-duty foil, sprayed with nonstick cooking spray

2 cups	cooked white rice	500 mL
1 cup	ready-to-use chicken broth	250 mL
4	cloves garlic, minced	4
3	shallots, finely chopped (about 3 tbsp/45 mL)	3
1	red bell pepper, finely chopped	1
1	can (14 oz/398 mL) kidney beans, drained and rinsed (see tip, at left)	1
1 tsp	dried thyme	5 mL
1 tsp	Creole seasoning	5 mL
8 oz	smoked andouille sausage, cut into ½-inch (1 cm) rounds	250 g
8 oz	large shrimp (26 to 30 count), peeled and deveined	250 g

1. In a medium bowl, combine rice and broth. Let stand for 5 minutes.

2. Meanwhile, in a small bowl, combine garlic, shallots, red pepper, beans, thyme and Creole seasoning, mixing well. Gently fold in sausage and shrimp.

3. Divide rice mixture evenly among prepared foil sheets and top with shrimp mixture. Fold foil into tent-style packets and seal edges tightly.

4. Place packets on preheated grill, cover and cook for 15 to 20 minutes, rotating packets occasionally, until shrimp are pink, firm and opaque.

Jambalaya with Sausage and Rice

This traditional Creole dish derives its combination of flavors and ingredients from Spanish and French influences. While there are many versions of jambalaya, including Cajun-style, this one is simple, bursting with flavor and great for grilling in foil.

Tip

After 25 minutes, remove one pouch from the grill and open it carefully to check whether the rice, shrimp and chicken are done. If not, close the pouch, return it to the grill and continue to cook, checking every 5 minutes, until done.

- Preheat barbecue grill to medium-high heat
- 2 double sheets heavy-duty foil, top sheets sprayed with nonstick cooking spray

8 oz	large shrimp (26 to 30 count), peeled and deveined, tail on	250 g
4 oz	boneless skinless chicken breast, cut into 1-inch (2.5 cm) pieces	125 g
3 oz	dry-cured chorizo sausage, sliced	90 g
2	small tomatoes, diced	2
2	cloves garlic, minced	2
1	small onion, finely chopped	1
1	green bell pepper, finely chopped	1
1	stalk celery, diced	1
1½ tbsp	Creole seasoning	22 mL
1 cup	instant brown rice	250 mL
½ cup	ready-to-use chicken broth	125 mL
	Kosher salt and freshly ground black pepper	

1. In a large bowl, combine shrimp, chicken, chorizo, tomatoes, garlic, onion, green pepper, celery, Creole seasoning, rice and broth. Season with salt and pepper, tossing to coat evenly.

2. Divide shrimp mixture evenly between prepared foil sheets. Fold foil into flat packets and seal edges tightly.

3. Place packets on preheated grill and cook for 25 minutes, rotating packets occasionally, until rice is tender, shrimp is pink, firm and opaque and chicken is no longer pink inside. Transfer jambalaya to a serving bowl.

Variation

For a Cajun version, use dried Cajun seasoning instead of Creole. You may want to omit the tomatoes, as early Cajun dishes likely did not include them, and use an additional ¼ cup (60 mL) ready-to-use chicken broth. However, any combination of ingredients that suits you is just fine, as this dish has many variations.

Quick and Easy Chicken Sausage Gumbo

Makes 6 servings

This version of a gumbo bathes your senses with the traditional taste of the classic Cajun stew but without the gravy-like consistency. Serve with cornbread for an authentic Cajun meal.

Tips

A typical rotisserie chicken weighs about 2½ lbs (1.25 kg) and will yield about 4 cups (1 L) shredded chicken.

Pick up your rotisserie chicken at the end of your grocery shopping trip. Use it within 2 hours or refrigerate and use within 3 days.

- Preheat barbecue grill to medium heat
- 6 sheets heavy-duty foil, sprayed with nonstick cooking spray

4	cloves garlic, minced	4
2	red bell peppers, chopped	2
1	onion, chopped	1
1	package (10 oz/300 g) frozen cut okra	1
1 tsp	dried oregano	5 mL
2 tbsp	vegetable oil	30 mL
	Kosher salt and freshly ground black pepper	
1	rotisserie chicken, deboned, skin removed and meat shredded	1
8 oz	smoked andouille sausage, cut into 1-inch (2.5 cm) slices, slices halved	250 g
½ cup	ready-to-use chicken broth	125 mL
1 tbsp	all-purpose flour	15 mL

1. In a large bowl, combine garlic, red peppers, onion, okra, oregano and oil. Season to taste with salt and pepper. Stir in chicken and sausage.

2. Measure broth in a glass measuring cup and gradually whisk in flour. Pour over gumbo mixture and toss well to combine.

3. Divide gumbo mixture evenly among prepared foil sheets. Fold foil into tent-style packets and seal edges tightly.

4. Place packets on preheated grill, cover and cook for 12 to 15 minutes, turning packets over often, until vegetables are tender-crisp.

Backyard Mexican Chicken and Corn Packets

Makes 6 servings

Here, chicken, beans and vegetables are seasoned with a flavorful spice blend that takes these packets to whole new level of deliciousness.

Tips

A typical rotisserie chicken weighs about 2½ lbs (1.25 kg) and will yield about 4 cups (1L) shredded chicken.

Pick up your rotisserie chicken at the end of your grocery shopping trip. Use it within 2 hours or refrigerate and use within 3 days.

If you can only find larger cans of black beans, you'll need 1½ cups (375 mL) drained beans for this recipe.

You can substitute ¾ cup (175 mL) thawed frozen corn for the canned corn.

- Preheat barbecue grill to medium heat
- 6 sheets heavy-duty foil, sprayed with nonstick cooking spray

1 tbsp	paprika	15 mL
1 tbsp	chili powder	15 mL
1 tsp	onion powder	5 mL
1 tsp	garlic powder	5 mL
1 tsp	ground cumin	5 mL
Pinch	freshly ground black pepper	Pinch
Pinch	cayenne pepper	Pinch
1	rotisserie chicken, deboned, skin removed and meat shredded	1
1	can (14 oz/398 mL) black beans, drained and rinsed (see tip, at left)	1
1	can (14 oz/398 mL) diced tomatoes, drained	1
1	can (14 oz/398 mL) corn, drained	1
¾ cup	shredded Monterey Jack and Cheddar cheese blend	175 mL
3	green onions, sliced (optional)	3

1. In a small bowl, combine paprika, chili powder, onion powder, garlic powder, cumin, black pepper and cayenne.

2. In a large bowl, combine chicken, beans, tomatoes, corn and spice blend, mixing well.

3. Divide chicken mixture evenly among prepared foil sheets. Fold foil into tent-style packets and seal edges tightly.

4. Place packets on preheated grill, cover and cook for 12 to 15 minutes, turning packets over often, until heated through. Serve sprinkled with cheese and green onions (if using).

"Brick-Oven" Mediterranean Chicken Pizza

When you don't have a brick oven in your backyard, the next best thing is to cook a foil-wrapped pizza on the grill. Layered with white sauce, chicken, artichokes and cheese, this pizza delivers Mediterranean flavors in the comfort of home.

Tips

If using rectangular flatbreads, 7- by 5-inch (18 by 13 cm) slices work best.

A typical rotisserie chicken weighs about 2½ lbs (1.25 kg) and will yield about 4 cups (1 L) shredded chicken.

Pick up your rotisserie chicken at the end of your grocery shopping trip. Use it within 2 hours or refrigerate and use within 3 days.

- Preheat barbecue grill to medium-high heat
- 4 sheets heavy-duty foil, sprayed with nonstick cooking spray

4	6-inch (15 cm) round flatbread slices (see tip, at left)	4
2 tbsp	virgin olive oil	30 mL
1 cup	white pizza sauce	250 mL
1⅓ cups	shredded mozzarella cheese, divided	325 mL
1	can (14 oz/398 mL) artichoke hearts, coarsely chopped	1
1½ cups	shredded rotisserie chicken	375 mL
2 tsp	dried oregano	10 mL
2 tsp	dried basil	10 mL

1. Place a slice of flatbread on each prepared foil sheet and brush with oil. Using the back of a spoon, spread one-quarter of sauce over each flatbread, then sprinkle with 2 to 3 tbsp (30 to 45 mL) cheese. Arrange artichokes and chicken on top, dividing evenly. Sprinkle with oregano and basil, then with the remaining cheese. Fold foil into tent-style packets and seal edges tightly.

2. Place packets on preheated grill and cook for 8 to 10 minutes, making a quarter-turn halfway through, until cheese is melted. Check often and remove flatbread from the grill before it starts to char.

Variations

Replace the artichoke hearts with 2 sliced yellow summer squash.

Sliced black olives, anchovies and chopped onion are delicious Mediterranean-style additions to this pizza.

Zesty Cilantro Lime Grilled Chicken

These grilled chicken packets are bursting with a range of flavors, and you can easily adjust the seasonings in each packet to please dinner guests with different preferences.

Tip

If you prefer this dish less spicy, discard some or all of the jalapeño seeds.

- Preheat barbecue grill to medium-high heat
- Meat mallet
- 4 sheets heavy-duty foil, sprayed with nonstick cooking spray

4	boneless skinless chicken breasts (each about 4 oz/125 g)	4
2 tbsp	butter, melted	30 mL
	Kosher salt and freshly ground black pepper	
1	clove garlic, minced	1
1	jalapeño pepper, sliced crosswise	1
1	red bell pepper, cut into ½-inch (1 cm) strips	1
1	small onion, sliced crosswise and rings separated	1
	Juice of 1 lime	
	Chopped fresh cilantro	

1. Place chicken breasts between 2 sheets of plastic wrap on a cutting board. Using the meat mallet, pound chicken to an even ½-inch (1 cm) thickness.

2. Discard plastic wrap and place a chicken breast on each prepared foil sheet. Brush both sides of chicken with butter and season with salt and pepper. Sprinkle with garlic and top with jalapeño, red pepper and onion, dividing evenly. Sprinkle with lime juice and cilantro. Fold foil into tent-style packets and seal edges tightly.

3. Place packets on preheated grill and cook for 10 to 15 minutes or until chicken is no longer pink inside.

Variations

To vary the seasoning for different diners, substitute chopped fresh thyme, sage or oregano for the cilantro.

You can easily add rice to this dish. Combine 2 cups (500 mL) instant white rice and 2 cups (500 mL) warm water. Fold foil up into a bowl shape. Divide rice mixture evenly among prepared foil sheets before adding the chicken. Nestle chicken on top of the rice.

Belgian-Style Marinated Chicken with Pub Mustard

Marinating these chicken breasts for hours with ale and herbs makes them deliciously tender and flavorful. The special pub mustard adds a zesty finish.

Tip

If you prefer not to use ale, you can substitute 1½ cups (375 mL) additional ready-to-use chicken broth plus 2 tsp (10 mL) balsamic vinegar.

• 4 sheets heavy-duty foil, sprayed with nonstick cooking spray

3	cloves garlic, minced	3
2 tbsp	chopped fresh parsley	30 mL
½ tsp	freshly ground black pepper	2 mL
1	bottle (12 oz/341 mL) ale	1
4	boneless skinless chicken breasts (each about 4 oz/125 g)	4
1 cup	ready-to-use chicken broth, divided	250 mL
1½ tbsp	sweet hot mustard	22 mL

1. In a small glass baking dish, combine garlic, parsley, pepper and ale. Add chicken and some of the broth if needed to completely cover chicken. Cover with plastic wrap and refrigerate for at least 2 hours or up to 8 hours.

2. Preheat barbecue grill to medium-high heat.

3. Remove chicken from marinade, reserving marinade, and place 1 breast on each prepared foil sheet. Fold foil into flat packets and seal edges tightly.

4. Strain marinade and pour into a small skillet. Add any remaining broth and bring to a boil over medium-high heat. Reduce heat to medium and cook, stirring occasionally, for 12 to 15 minutes or until liquid is reduced by two-thirds. Reduce heat to medium-low and stir in mustard; simmer, stirring, for 3 to 4 minutes or until thickened.

5. Meanwhile, place packets on grill and cook for 10 to 15 minutes or until chicken is no longer pink inside.

6. Transfer chicken to serving plates and drizzle with pub mustard.

Italian Parmesan Chicken with Green Beans

This grilled chicken with Italian sauce is so moist, tender and delicious, you will want to always wrap your chicken breasts in foil for perfect results.

Tips

Serve over a bed of cooked fettucine for a hearty Italian feast.

Garnish with toasted sliced almonds for a nutty and crunchy finish.

- Preheat barbecue grill to medium heat
- Meat mallet
- 4 sheets heavy-duty foil, sprayed with nonstick cooking spray

4	boneless skinless chicken breasts (each about 3 oz/90 g)	4
1	package (16 oz/500 g) frozen green beans	1
1 cup	marinara sauce	250 mL
¼ cup	freshly grated Parmesan cheese	60 mL
1 cup	shredded mozzarella cheese	250 mL

1. Place chicken breasts between 2 sheets of plastic wrap on a cutting board. Using the meat mallet, pound chicken to an even thickness.

2. Discard plastic wrap and place a chicken breast on each prepared foil sheet. Top with green beans and marinara sauce, dividing evenly. Sprinkle with Parmesan. Fold foil into tent-style packets and seal edges tightly.

3. Place packets on preheated grill, cover and cook for 15 to 20 minutes or until chicken is no longer pink inside. Serve sprinkled with mozzarella.

Ready-to-Go Breakfast
Tacos (page 25)

Mandarin Orange Chicken and Broccoli (page 35)

Peach and Ginger–Glazed Pork Chops (page 36)
with Cheesy Chive Green Beans (page 59)

Beef-Stuffed Pepper
Boats (page 51)

Pineapple Upside-Down Cakes (page 62)

Lemon Dill Rainbow Trout with
Carrots and Fennel (page 86)

Portugese Clam Bake with
Corn on the Cob (page 87)

Jambalaya with Sausage
and Rice (page 90)

Spicy Szechuan Grilled Chicken and Rice

Makes 4 servings

Turn up the heat with this spicy combination of chicken, vegetables and rice in an all-in-one meal packet.

Tips

A vegetable mix that features carrots will complement this dish wonderfully. A carrot and water chestnut mix is one of my favorites, as is a carrot, broccoli and cauliflower mix.

Eight boneless skinless chicken thighs can be used in place of the breasts. Increase the cooking time to 25 to 35 minutes or until juices run clear when chicken is pierced.

- Preheat barbecue grill to medium heat
- 4 sheets heavy-duty foil, sprayed with nonstick cooking spray

½ cup	instant brown rice	125 mL
½ cup	water	125 mL
1	package (10 oz/300 g) frozen mixed vegetables (see tip, at left), thawed	1
¼ cup	Szechuan sauce	60 mL
1½ tbsp	freshly squeezed lime juice	22 mL
4	boneless skinless chicken breasts (each about 4 oz/125 g)	4
¼ cup	chopped peanuts	60 mL

1. In a small bowl, combine rice and water. Let stand for 5 minutes, then stir in mixed vegetables.

2. In a small bowl or measuring cup, combine Szechuan sauce and lime juice.

3. Divide rice mixture evenly among prepared foil sheets. Nestle chicken on top of rice and drizzle sauce over top, dividing evenly. Fold foil into tent-style packets and seal edges tightly.

4. Place packets on preheated grill, cover and cook for 20 to 30 minutes, rotating packets a half-turn halfway through, until chicken is no longer pink inside. Serve sprinkled with peanuts.

Wasabi Plum Chicken with Peppers

Your taste buds will tingle with excitement when they experience this delectable combination of sweet, tangy and spicy glazed chicken.

Tips

You can vary the spice level of the sauce by using more or less wasabi.

For a gluten-free version, substitute liquid amino acids for the soy sauce.

- Preheat barbecue grill to medium heat
- 4 sheets heavy-duty foil, sprayed with nonstick cooking spray

2 tsp	minced gingerroot	10 mL
¼ cup	plum sauce	60 mL
1 tbsp	soy sauce	15 mL
1 tsp	prepared wasabi (or to taste)	5 mL
1	red bell pepper, cut into ½-inch (1 cm) strips	1
1	green bell pepper, cut into ½-inch (1 cm) strips	1
1 tbsp	virgin olive oil	15 mL
	Kosher salt and freshly ground black pepper	
4	boneless skinless chicken breasts (each about 4 oz/125 g)	4

1. In a small bowl, combine ginger, plum sauce, soy sauce and wasabi.

2. Divide red and green peppers evenly among prepared foil sheets. Drizzle with oil and season with salt and pepper. Top each with a chicken breast and drizzle with sauce. Fold foil into tent-style packets and seal edges tightly.

3. Place packets on preheated grill, cover and cook for 20 to 30 minutes, rotating packets halfway through, until chicken is no longer pink inside.

Comfort Chicken and Parsnips with Mole Sauce

The sweet, spicy and fruity flavors of a rich, dark mole sauce meld decadently with tender chicken and sweet parsnips. Savory and simple to prepare, this dish is one you will definitely want to try.

Tip

For ease in transferring the packets to the grill, place them on a rimless baking sheet and slide them off the baking sheet onto the grill.

- Preheat barbecue grill to medium heat
- 4 sheets heavy-duty foil, sprayed with nonstick cooking spray

1 lb	boneless skinless chicken breasts, cut into strips	500 g
3	parsnips, sliced	3
1 cup	mole sauce	250 mL
2 cups	cooked brown rice	500 mL
	Chopped fresh cilantro (optional)	

1. Divide chicken evenly among prepared foil sheets and top with parsnips. Pour mole sauce over top, dividing evenly. Arrange rice alongside chicken, dividing evenly. Fold foil into tent-style packets and seal edges tightly.

2. Place packets on preheated grill, cover and cook for 15 to 20 minutes or until chicken is no longer pink inside. Serve sprinkled with cilantro, if desired.

Variation

Reduce the brown rice to 1 cup (250 mL) and serve the finished dish wrapped in tortillas.

Tomato Basil Chicken and Asparagus

A creamy tomato soup infuses these packets with flavor, for a satisfying, quick and easy weeknight meal.

Tip

If you have leftover rotisserie chicken on hand, you can substitute 2 cups (500 mL) shredded chicken for the chicken breast cubes. Reduce the cooking time to 8 to 12 minutes.

- Preheat barbecue grill to medium heat
- 4 sheets heavy-duty foil, sprayed with nonstick cooking spray

1	can (10 oz/284 mL) condensed tomato soup	1
1 cup	milk	250 mL
1 lb	boneless skinless chicken breasts, cut into 1-inch (2.5 cm) cubes	500 g
16	asparagus spears (about 8 oz/250 g), trimmed and cut into 2-inch (5 cm) pieces	16
8 oz	mushrooms, sliced	250 g
	Kosher salt and freshly ground black pepper	
	Fresh basil leaves (optional)	

1. In a small bowl, combine tomato soup and milk.

2. Divide chicken, asparagus and mushrooms evenly among prepared foil packets. Pour soup mixture over top. Season with salt and pepper. Fold foil into tent-style packets and seal edges tightly.

3. Place packets on preheated grill and cook for 15 to 20 minutes, turning packets over once, until chicken is no longer pink inside. Serve garnished with basil, if desired.

Fiery Pineapple Chicken and Roasted Cauliflower

Makes 4 servings

Quick and easy preparation and cleanup are the trademarks of these spicy, savory and sweet chicken packets with tropical flair.

Tip
You can substitute other fruit preserves and fresh fruit for the pineapple preserves and chunks. Peaches, apples and apricots all work well.

- Preheat barbecue grill to medium heat
- 4 sheets heavy-duty foil, sprayed with nonstick cooking spray

2 tbsp	packed brown sugar	30 mL
¼ tsp	hot pepper flakes	1 mL
⅓ cup	pineapple preserves	75 mL
1 tbsp	soy sauce	15 mL
1 lb	boneless skinless chicken breasts, cut into 2-inch (5 cm) pieces	500 g
1	red bell pepper, cut into 1½-inch (4 cm) pieces	1
1	green bell pepper, cut into 1½-inch (4 cm) pieces	1
1 cup	pineapple chunks	250 mL
¼ tsp	salt	1 mL

1. In a small bowl, combine brown sugar, hot pepper flakes, pineapple preserves and soy sauce.

2. Divide chicken, red pepper, green pepper and pineapple evenly among prepared foil sheets. Sprinkle with salt. Fold foil into tent-style packets and seal edges tightly.

3. Place packets on preheated grill, cover and cook for 15 to 18 minutes, turning packets over once halfway through, until chicken is no longer pink inside.

Glazed Bacon-Wrapped Chicken and Baby Portobellos

Bacon lovers, get ready for an infusion of bacon-wrapped chicken, onions, peppers and mushrooms that will ignite your taste buds.

Tips

Always wear disposable kitchen gloves when handling hot peppers.

If you would prefer less heat, remove the seeds from the jalapeño.

You can remove the skin from the chicken thighs if you prefer (or just purchase skinless thighs).

Boneless skinless chicken breasts can be used in place of the thighs. Reduce the cooking time to 25 to 30 minutes or until chicken is no longer pink inside.

- Preheat barbecue grill to medium heat
- 4 sheets heavy-duty foil, sprayed with nonstick cooking spray

8	slices bacon	8
2	large onions, sliced	2
1	small jalapeño pepper, sliced (optional)	1
8 oz	baby portobello (cremini) mushrooms, sliced	250 g
2 tsp	garlic powder	10 mL
	Kosher salt and freshly ground black pepper	
4	boneless skin-on chicken thighs (each about 4 oz/125 g)	4
1 cup	sweet barbecue sauce	250 mL

1. Place 2 bacon slices on each prepared foil sheet. Top with onions, jalapeño and mushrooms, dividing evenly. Sprinkle with garlic powder and season with salt and pepper. Place a chicken thigh on top of the vegetables in each packet. Wrap bacon slices around chicken and vegetables, tucking in ends as needed. Drizzle with barbecue sauce. Fold foil into flat packets and seal edges tightly.

2. Place packets on preheated grill and cook for 30 to 40 minutes or until juices run clear when chicken is pierced and bacon is tender-crisp.

Fiery Chilean Chicken with Roasted Tomatoes

If you like it spicy, this dish will make you swoon. Grilled seasoned tomatoes and chicken are topped with a fiery glaze that will make you feel like dancing the Chilean cueca.

Tip

If you love roasted tomatoes, you can follow step 2 and cook tomatoes in a separate foil packet for a great side dish anytime. Cook for 20 to 30 minutes or until done to your liking.

- Preheat barbecue grill to medium-high heat
- 4 sheets heavy-duty foil, sprayed with nonstick cooking spray

½ cup	granulated sugar	125 mL
2 tsp	ancho chile powder	10 mL
2 tsp	chipotle chile powder	10 mL
1 tsp	ground cumin	5 mL
1½ cups	water	375 mL
⅓ cup	dry white wine	75 mL
⅓ cup	soy sauce	75 mL
⅓ cup	balsamic vinegar	75 mL
8	small tomatoes (about 1 lb/500 g total), cut in half	8
2 tbsp	virgin olive oil	30 mL
2	cloves garlic, minced	2
4	sprigs fresh rosemary	4
	Kosher salt and freshly ground black pepper	
4	boneless skinless chicken thighs (each about 4 oz/125 g)	4
	Sour cream (optional)	
3 tbsp	coarsely chopped fresh cilantro leaves (optional)	45 mL

1. In a medium saucepan, combine sugar, ancho chile powder, chipotle chile powder, cumin, water, wine, soy sauce and vinegar. Bring to a boil over medium-high heat. Reduce heat and simmer for 10 to 15 minutes or until thickened.

2. Place 4 tomato halves, cut side up, on each prepared foil sheet. Drizzle with oil and sprinkle with garlic. Top each with a rosemary sprig. Season with salt and pepper.

3. Place a chicken thigh on top of the tomatoes in each packet and drizzle with chile sauce. Fold foil into flat packets and seal edges tightly.

4. Place packets on preheated grill, cover and cook for 20 to 30 minutes, rotating packets a half-turn halfway through, until chicken is no longer pink inside. If desired, serve dolloped with sour cream and garnished with cilantro.

Southern-Style Baby Back Ribs and Seasoned Potato Wedges

These sweet and sassy ribs are cooked to melt-in-your-mouth perfection. The crispy seasoned wedges are the perfect complement to this backyard feast.

Tip

Use a baking sheet to help you transfer the packets to and from the grill.

- Preheat barbecue grill to medium heat
- 4 double sheets heavy-duty foil, top sheets sprayed with nonstick cooking spray

Ribs

1 tbsp	kosher salt	15 mL
1 tbsp	paprika	15 mL
2 tsp	garlic powder	10 mL
1½ tsp	Montreal steak seasoning	7 mL
3 lbs	baby back pork ribs, cut into 2 slabs	1.5 kg
2 tbsp	packed brown sugar	30 mL
½ cup	unsweetened apple juice	125 mL
1 cup	barbecue sauce	250 mL

Potatoes

8	red-skinned potatoes (about 1 lb/500 g), cut into wedges	8
2 tbsp	virgin olive oil	30 mL
1	packet (1 oz/28 g) dry onion soup mix	1

1. *Ribs:* In a small bowl, combine salt, paprika, garlic powder and steak seasoning. Rub mixture into both sides of ribs. Place a slab of ribs on each of 2 prepared foil sheets. Fold edges of foil up into a bowl shape around the ribs.

2. In the same bowl, combine brown sugar and apple juice. Pour into packets, dividing evenly. Fold foil into tent-style packets and seal edges tightly.

3. Place packets on preheated grill and cook for 1 hour or until meat is tender. Open packets with caution, allowing steam to escape, and brush tops of ribs with barbecue sauce. Leaving packets open, cook for 15 minutes or until sauce is sticky.

Tip

Serve with additional barbecue sauce for dipping the ribs and a side of ketchup or ranch dressing for dipping the potato wedges.

4. *Potatoes:* Meanwhile, in a large sealable plastic bag, combine potatoes, oil and onion soup mix. Seal and shake to coat. Divide potatoes evenly among the remaining prepared foil sheets. Fold foil into tent-style packets and seal edges tightly.

5. When ribs have cooked for 40 minutes, place potato packets on grill. Grill for 35 minutes, turning packets over occasionally, until potatoes are tender-crisp. Serve with ribs.

Pork Tenderloin with Summer Squash

Makes 6 servings

This zesty combination of pork medallions and summer vegetables cooks to moist and tender perfection every time.

Tips

When checking for doneness, remove one packet to a plate and carefully open the top, allowing steam to escape. If more cooking time is needed, reseal the packet and return it to the grill.

Prepare individual packets with the preferred ingredients of individual diners and use a black marker to write the name of the person and their preferred doneness on the packet. Cook and serve accordingly.

- Preheat barbecue grill to medium-high heat
- 6 sheets heavy-duty foil, sprayed with nonstick cooking spray

⅓ cup	packed brown sugar	75 mL
2 tsp	minced garlic	10 mL
1 tsp	kosher salt	5 mL
1 tsp	paprika	5 mL
½ tsp	hot pepper flakes	2 mL
2 lbs	pork tenderloin, cut into 1-inch (2.5 cm) medallions	1 kg
2	zucchini, sliced	2
1	yellow summer squash, sliced	1
1	large onion, sliced	1
1	small bulb fennel, sliced	1
2 tsp	freshly squeezed lemon juice	10 mL
2 tbsp	virgin olive oil	30 mL
	Kosher salt and freshly ground black pepper	

1. In a small bowl, combine brown sugar, garlic, salt, paprika and hot pepper flakes. Rub mixture generously onto pork medallions. Divide pork evenly among prepared foil sheets.

2. In a large bowl, toss together zucchini, yellow squash, onion, fennel, lemon juice and oil. Spoon over pork medallions, dividing evenly. Season with salt and pepper. Fold foil into tent-style packets and seal edges tightly.

3. Place packets on preheated grill, cover and cook for 22 to 24 minutes, rotating packets a half-turn halfway through, until just a hint of pink remains in pork (or cook to desired doneness). Remove packets from grill and let rest, without opening, for 3 minutes before serving.

Tahitian Pineapple Ham

Makes 4 servings

While not quite like being in the South Pacific, the tropical flavors of these juicy and sweet ham packets may have you believing you've been transported there.

Tips

Canned sweet potatoes are often labeled "yams" though they are not, in fact, yams at all.

If you would like to serve this meal directly out of the packets, make it easier to eat by using 12 oz (375 g) cubed cooked ham.

- Preheat barbecue grill to medium heat
- 4 sheets heavy-duty foil, sprayed with nonstick cooking spray

4	½-inch (1 cm) thick slices cooked ham	4
4	pineapple rings	4
1	can (15 oz/444 mL) chopped sweet potatoes in heavy syrup, drained	1
¼ cup	orange juice	60 mL
3 tbsp	butter, cut into small pieces	45 mL

1. Place a slice of ham and a slice of pineapple on each prepared foil sheet. Top with sweet potatoes and orange juice, dividing evenly. Dot butter on top. Fold foil into flat packets and seal edges tightly.

2. Place packets on preheated grill and cook for 20 minutes or until heated through.

Zesty Pork Pita Pockets

Ground pork gets an exhilarating treatment in these spicy pita pockets, grilled to perfection.

Tips

These pita sandwiches are excellent served with a side salad of vegetables or fruit.

For ease in transferring the packets to the grill, place them on a rimless baking sheet and slide them off the baking sheet onto the grill.

- Preheat barbecue grill to medium heat
- 3 sheets heavy-duty foil, sprayed with nonstick cooking spray

1 lb	ground pork	500 g
1	onion, chopped	1
1	tomato, chopped	1
2 tbsp	chopped fresh cilantro	30 mL
1 tsp	ground cumin	5 mL
½ tsp	chili powder	2 mL
½ tsp	kosher salt	2 mL
½ tsp	freshly ground black pepper	2 mL
3	6-inch (15 cm) pitas	3
1 tbsp	virgin olive oil	15 mL

1. In a large bowl, combine pork, onion, tomato, cilantro, cumin, chili powder, salt and pepper.

2. Carefully open each pita at one end and fill evenly with one-third of the pork mixture. Brush outsides of pitas with oil. Place a stuffed pita on each prepared foil sheet. Fold foil into flat packets and seal edges tightly.

3. Place packets on preheated grill, cover and cook for 18 to 22 minutes, rotating packets a quarter-turn occasionally, until pork is no longer pink and pitas are lightly browned. Cut pitas into quarters and serve 2 slices per person.

Variation
Substitute ground chicken or turkey for the pork.

Backyard Kielbasa and Gnocchi with Marinara Sauce

Makes 4 servings

Here, the lovely pillowy dumplings known as gnocchi are paired with kielbasa and then covered in a garlicky basil tomato sauce for a mouthwatering meal.

Tips

Frozen gnocchi works best in this recipe. The dry, shelf-stable gnocchi will not cook up as well here.

If you don't use the whole package of gnocchi, the opened package can be refrigerated and used within 3 days.

To cut basil into chiffonade, stack the leaves and roll them into a tight roll. Cut crosswise into 1/8-inch (3 mm) slices and unfurl the slices.

- Preheat barbecue grill to medium heat
- 4 sheets heavy-duty foil, sprayed with nonstick cooking spray

1	package (12 oz/375 g) frozen gnocchi	1
1	onion, chopped	1
1	clove garlic, minced	1
	Kosher salt and freshly ground black pepper	
1 tbsp	olive oil	15 mL
1 lb	kielbasa, cut into 2-inch (5 cm) slices	500 g
1	jar (26 oz/740 mL) marinara sauce	1
2 tbsp	fresh basil, cut into chiffonade or roughly chopped	30 mL
	Freshly grated Parmesan cheese (optional)	

1. Divide gnocchi, onion and garlic evenly among prepared foil sheets. Season with salt and pepper and drizzle with oil. Top with kielbasa and marinara sauce, dividing evenly. Sprinkle with basil. Fold foil into flat packets and seal edges tightly.

2. Place packets on preheated grill, cover and cook for 25 to 30 minutes or until gnocchi are tender and all ingredients are heated through. If desired, serve sprinkle with Parmesan.

Variation

Replace the gnocchi with 2 cups (500 mL) cubed russet potatoes.

Home Run Hot Dog and Red Potato Packets

In this twist on a summertime ballgame favorite, hot dogs and potatoes get a flavorful cheesy treatment.

Tip

For ease in transferring the packets to the grill, place them on a rimless baking sheet and slide them off the baking sheet onto the grill.

- Preheat barbecue grill to medium heat
- 4 sheets heavy-duty foil, sprayed with nonstick cooking spray

1¼ lbs	red-skinned potatoes (unpeeled), cut into thin wedges	625 g
4	frankfurters, cut into 1-inch (2.5 cm) pieces	4
1	small onion, sliced	1
¼ cup	shredded Cheddar cheese	60 mL
½ cup	honey mustard	125 mL

1. Divide potatoes evenly among prepared foil sheets. Top with frankfurters, onion and cheese, dividing evenly. Drizzle with honey mustard. Fold foil into flat packets and seal edges tightly.

2. Place packets on preheated grill, cover and cook for 20 to 24 minutes or until potatoes are tender and frankfurters are heated through.

Variation

Leave the frankfurters whole. After cooking, transfer the franks to hot dog buns and serve with potatoes on the side.

Sassy Grilled Beef Roast with Orange-Glazed Carrots

When you open this grilled beef packet, the smell will tell you are in for a treat, and one look at the dreamy orange-ginger glaze blanketing the carrots and steak will confirm it.

Tips

Use a baking sheet to help you transfer the heavy packet to and from the grill.

You may want to rotate the packet a quarter-turn a couple of times to avoid any hot spots.

Beef chuck roast becomes more tender and full-flavored when cooked to medium instead of medium-rare. Cooking it closer to well done, however, can make it tougher.

- Preheat barbecue grill to medium-low heat
- Large double sheet heavy-duty foil, top sheet sprayed with nonstick cooking spray

1 tsp	minced gingerroot	5 mL
⅓ cup	orange juice	75 mL
¼ cup	orange marmalade	60 mL
1 tbsp	Worcestershire sauce	15 mL
1½ lb	boneless center cut beef chuck roast	750 g
1	packet (1 oz/28 g) dry onion soup mix	1
6	carrots, cut in half lengthwise, then quartered	6

1. In a glass measuring cup, combine ginger, orange juice, marmalade and Worcestershire sauce.

2. Place roast in center of prepared foil sheet and sprinkle with onion soup mix. Add carrots on top of and around roast. Pour ginger mixture over top. Fold foil into a tent-style packet and seal edges tightly.

3. Place packet on preheated grill, cover and cook for about 30 minutes, or until an instant-read thermometer inserted in the thickest part of the roast registers 160°F (71°C) for medium (or cook to desired doneness) Remove packet from grill and let rest, without opening for 10 minutes.

4. Transfer roast to a cutting board and slice across the grain. Serve with carrots.

Sweet-and-Spicy Tri-Tip with Brown Sugar Baby Carrots

Marinating this roast overnight gives the zesty rub the opportunity to infuse it with marvelous flavor. The grill adds a mouthwatering glazed sear.

Tip

Wear kitchen gloves when rubbing the chipotle mixture into the roast, so as not to burn your hands.

- Large double sheet heavy-duty foil, top sheet sprayed with nonstick cooking spray

3	cloves garlic, minced	3
1	chipotle pepper in adobo sauce, minced	1
½ cup	packed light brown sugar, divided	125 mL
	Grated zest and juice of 1 lime	
1½ to 2 lb	beef tri-tip roast	750 g to 1 kg
1	onion, sliced	1
	Kosher salt and freshly ground black pepper	
1 lb	baby carrots	500 g

1. In a medium bowl, combine garlic, chipotle, all but 1 tbsp (15 mL) of the brown sugar, lime zest and lime juice. Rub mixture all over roast. Place roast in a large sealable plastic bag, seal and refrigerate for at least 6 hours or up to 24 hours.

2. Preheat barbecue grill to medium-high heat.

3. Arrange onion slices in a single layer on prepared foil sheet. Remove the roast from the bag and place on top of the onions; discard any excess marinade. Season roast on both sides with salt and pepper. Fold foil into a flat packet and seal edges tightly.

4. Place packet on grill and cook for 16 to 20 minutes, turning packet over halfway through, until an instant-read thermometer inserted in the thickest part of the roast registers 135°F (57°C) for medium-rare (or cook to desired doneness, keeping in mind that the meat continues to cook in step 5). Remove packet from grill and open carefully so as not to tear the foil.

Tip

Use a baking sheet to help you transfer the heavy packet to and from the grill.

5. Remove roast from foil, saving juices in foil, and place roast directly on grill for 4 to 6 minutes, turning once, to sear the meat to your liking. Transfer to a cutting board, tent with foil and let rest for 10 minutes (or until carrots are done).

6. Meanwhile, add carrots to the reserved foil, fold foil into a tent-style packet and seal edges tightly. Place packet on grill and cook for 15 to 20 minutes or until carrots are tender-crisp.

7. Slice roast across the grain and serve with carrots.

Variation

Add 6 to 8 yellow-fleshed potatoes (about 1 lb/500 g), cut into 1-inch (2.5 cm) cubes, with the carrots.

Mediterranean Marinated Skirt Steak and Vegetables

The juicy seasoned steak grilled alongside a marinated Mediterranean vegetable combination is a pleasurable pairing of contrasting flavors.

Tip

For a little bit of heat, add 2 tsp (10 mL) hot pepper flakes with the vinegar in step 3.

- 2 double sheets heavy-duty foil, top sheets sprayed with nonstick cooking spray

4	small red-skinned potatoes, cut into chunks	4
1	zucchini, cut into 1-inch (2.5 cm) pieces	1
1	yellow summer squash, cut into 1-inch (2.5 cm) pieces	1
1	red onion, thinly sliced	1
1	bulb fennel, cut into thin wedges	1
1	bottle (16 oz/475 mL) Greek vinaigrette	1
2	sprigs fresh rosemary (optional)	2
2 tbsp	virgin olive oil	30 mL
2 tbsp	balsamic vinegar	30 mL
1 lb	beef skirt steak, cut in half	500 g
	Kosher salt and freshly ground black pepper	

1. In a large sealable plastic bag, combine potatoes, zucchini, yellow squash, onion, fennel and dressing. Seal, toss to coat and marinate at room temperature for 2 hours.

2. Preheat barbecue grill to medium-high heat.

3. In another large sealable plastic bag, combine rosemary (if using), oil and vinegar. Add steak, seal and toss to coat.

4. Using a slotted spoon, transfer one-quarter of the marinated vegetables to each prepared foil sheet. Remove steak from oil mixture, discarding oil mixture, and place on top of vegetables. Season with salt and pepper. Top steak with the remaining vegetables, dividing evenly. Reserve vegetable marinade. Fold foil into flat packets and seal edges tightly.

Tip

For a quick and easy version, use a 16-oz (500 g) or larger bag of thawed frozen mixed Mediterranean vegetables.

5. Place packets on grill and cook for 12 to 16 minutes, turning packets over once, until an instant-read thermometer inserted in the thickest part of the steak registers 145°F (63°C) for medium-rare (or cook to desired doneness). Remove from grill and let rest for 3 minutes before opening foil.

6. Meanwhile, in a small saucepan, heat the reserved vegetable marinade over medium heat until steaming.

7. Transfer steak to a cutting board and thinly slice on the bias across the grain. Serve with vegetables, drizzled with warm marinade.

Rosemary Thyme Steak and Asparagus

Makes 2 servings

Rosemary and thyme pair beautifully on seasoned grilled steak with a side of lemon asparagus, creating an all-in-one meal that is truly a special treat.

Tips

If you prefer other steak cuts, you can use them in place of the ribeyes. The steaks should be at least ½ inch (1 cm) thick and not more than ¾ inch (1.5 cm) thick so they will be done at the same time as the asparagus.

The internal temperature of the meat will rise slightly during the resting time.

- Preheat barbecue grill to medium-high heat
- 2 sheets heavy-duty foil, sprayed with nonstick cooking spray

1 tbsp	butter, cut into pieces	15 mL
2	beef ribeye steaks, about ½ inch (1 cm) thick	2
	Kosher salt and freshly ground black pepper	
2	sprigs fresh rosemary	2
4	sprigs fresh thyme	4
12	spears asparagus (about 8 oz/250 g)	12
2 tsp	olive oil	10 mL
1	lemon, cut into wedges	1

1. Dot 1 tsp (5 mL) butter near the center of each prepared foil sheet. Season both sides of steaks with salt and pepper and place on top of butter. Dot top of steaks with the remaining butter pieces. Place 1 rosemary sprig and 2 thyme sprigs on top of each steak.

2. Place 6 asparagus spears next to each steak. Drizzle asparagus with oil. Squeeze juice from lemon wedges over asparagus and season with salt. Fold foil into tent-style packets and seal edges tightly.

3. Place packets on preheated grill and cook for 8 to 10 minutes, turning packets over once, until asparagus is tender-crisp and an instant-read thermometer inserted in the thickest part of a steak registers 145°F (63°C) for medium-rare (or cook to desired doneness). Remove from grill and let rest for 5 minutes before opening foil.

Beer-Glazed Beef Steaks with Bacon and Onions

These juicy beef steaks are glazed with a barbecue ale sauce and then married with onions and bacon for an inexpensive steak that tastes anything but.

Tips

The steaks can be served on their own or on an onion or kaiser roll.

For a real treat, serve with Bacon Ranch Potato Bundles (page 125).

- Preheat barbecue grill to medium-low heat
- 4 sheets heavy-duty foil, sprayed with nonstick cooking spray

1	bottle (12 oz/341 mL) ale	1
½ cup	barbecue sauce	125 mL
4	beef sirloin cube or minute steaks (each about 5 oz/150 g)	4
	Kosher salt and freshly ground black pepper	
2	onions, thinly sliced	2
4	slices applewood-smoked bacon, cooked crisp and cut in half	4

1. In a large sealable plastic bag, combine ale and barbecue sauce. Season steaks with salt and pepper. Add steaks to bag, seal and refrigerate for at least 30 minutes or up to 2 hours.

2. Remove steaks from marinade, reserving marinade, and place 1 steak on each prepared foil sheet. Top with onions and bacon, dividing evenly. Fold edges of foil up into a bowl shape around the steak. Pour marinade over top. Fold foil into flat packets and seal edges tightly.

3. Place packets on preheated grill and cook for 5 minutes. Increase heat to medium and cook for 10 minutes or until beef is no longer pink inside.

Taco Burgers with Festive Pepper Hash Browns

Makes 6 servings

These all-in-one dinner packets deliver a flavorful combination of taco-flavored burgers, potatoes with peppers and onions, and a warm cheesy salsa.

Tips

The patties can be prepared through step 1 and frozen for up to 2 months. Thaw patties in the refrigerator before cooking.

Taco seasoning mix can be found in jars in the seasoning section of the grocery store. You can also purchase a 1.25-oz (35 g) packet and measure out the specified amount.

- Preheat barbecue grill to medium heat
- 6 sheets heavy-duty foil, sprayed with nonstick cooking spray

1½ lbs	80/20 (lean) ground beef	750 g
¾ cup	dry bread crumbs	175 mL
3 tbsp	taco seasoning mix	45 mL
⅓ cup	milk	75 mL
1	package (32 oz/908 g) frozen O'Brien potatoes	1
1 cup	salsa con queso	250 mL

1. In a medium bowl, combine beef, bread crumbs, taco seasoning and milk. Form into six ½-inch (1 cm) thick patties.

2. In a large bowl, combine potatoes and salsa con queso.

3. Place a patty on each prepared foil sheet. Top with potato mixture, dividing evenly. Fold foil into tent-style packets and seal edges tightly.

4. Place packets on preheated grill, cover and cook for 18 to 22 minutes, rotating packets a quarter-turn occasionally, until an instant-read thermometer inserted horizontally into the center of a patty registers 160°F (71°C).

Dinner-for-Two Herbed Lamb Chops and Asparagus

Herb- and garlic-crusted lamb and asparagus will make an elegant dinner for two very special.

Tips

Lamb chops are best when served medium-rare, 145°F (63°C). You can cook longer if you prefer your lamb more well done.

Serve with a side salad of mixed greens and your favorite dressing.

- Preheat barbecue grill to medium-high heat
- 2 sheets heavy-duty foil, sprayed with nonstick cooking spray

4	lamb chops, about ¾ inch (2 cm) thick	4
1 tbsp	virgin olive oil, divided	15 mL
1	small clove garlic, sliced	1
1 tbsp	dried herbes de Provence	15 mL
10	spears asparagus, trimmed, cut into 3-inch (7.5 cm) pieces	10
	Kosher salt	

1. Brush both sides of lamb chops with some of the oil. Place 2 lamb chops on each prepared foil sheet and cut a small slit in the top of each chop. Push garlic slices into slits. Sprinkle lamb with herbes de Provence. Arrange asparagus around chops, dividing evenly. Drizzle the remaining oil over asparagus. Season lamb and asparagus with salt. Fold foil into flat packets and seal edges tightly.

2. Place packets on preheated grill and cook for 5 to 7 minutes per side, turning packets over once, until asparagus is tender-crisp and an instant-read thermometer inserted in the thickest part of a lamb chop registers 145°F (63°C) for medium-rare (or cook to desired doneness).

Grilled Lamb and Vegetables with Cucumber Yogurt Sauce

This moist and tender grilled lamb is so delicious you won't want to make traditional kabobs anymore. Served with the cucumber yogurt dipping sauce, they are just spectacular.

- Preheat barbecue grill to medium-high heat
- 6 sheets heavy-duty foil, sprayed with nonstick cooking spray

1 lb	cubed trimmed boneless lamb shoulder or leg (about 1-inch/2.5 cm cubes)	500 g
2	cloves garlic, minced	2
1	red onion, cut into wedges and halved	1
1	small zucchini, cut into $\frac{1}{2}$-inch (1 cm) slices	1
1	small yellow summer squash, cut into $\frac{1}{2}$-inch (1 cm) slices	1
1	red bell pepper, cut into $\frac{1}{2}$-inch (1 cm) pieces	1
2 tbsp	fresh rosemary leaves	30 mL
2 tbsp	virgin olive oil	30 mL
	Kosher salt and freshly ground black pepper	

Cucumber Yogurt Sauce

$\frac{1}{2}$	cucumber, peeled, seeded and finely chopped	$\frac{1}{2}$
2 tsp	chopped fresh dill	10 mL
1 cup	plain Greek yogurt	250 mL
	Kosher salt and freshly ground black pepper	

1. In a large bowl, combine lamb, garlic, onion, zucchini, yellow squash, red pepper, rosemary and oil. Season with salt and pepper, tossing to coat evenly.

2. Divide lamb mixture evenly among prepared foil sheets. Fold foil into flat packets and seal edges tightly.

Tip

If desired, serve with small wooden skewers to make it easy and fun to dip the lamb cubes and vegetables into the sauce.

3. Place packets on preheated grill and cook for 8 to 10 minutes, turning packets over occasionally, until lamb is medium-rare (or cook to desired doneness).

4. *Sauce:* Meanwhile, in a small bowl, combine cucumber, dill and yogurt. Season to taste with salt and pepper.

5. Serve lamb mixture with dipping sauce.

Cheesy Scalloped Potato Packets

Makes 4 servings

Your favorite creamy, cheesy, buttery potatoes — a classic comfort-food side dish — can be made in individual serving packets on the grill with much less cleanup.

Tip

There are about 3 to 4 medium russet potatoes in 1 lb (500 g). Choose potatoes that are a similar size for even cooking and better presentation. Discard any green potatoes or potatoes with black sections.

- Preheat barbecue grill to medium heat
- 4 sheets heavy-duty foil, sprayed with nonstick cooking spray

4	russet potatoes (about 1 lb/250 g), peeled and thinly sliced	4
½ cup	freshly grated Parmesan cheese	125 mL
¼ cup	melted butter	60 mL
	Kosher salt and freshly ground black pepper	
½ cup	heavy or whipping (35%) cream	125 mL

1. In a large bowl, toss together potatoes, cheese and butter. Season with salt and pepper.

2. Arrange 4 to 5 layers of potatoes in a rectangle on each prepared foil sheet, dividing evenly. Fold edges of foil up into a bowl shape around the potatoes. Pour cream over potatoes, dividing evenly. Fold foil into tent-style packets and seal edges tightly.

3. Place packets on preheated grill and cook for 25 minutes, rotating a half-turn halfway through, until potatoes are tender.

Zesty Garlic Parmesan Red Potatoes

You will love this easy, savory potato dish with a golden Parmesan crust.

Tip

There are about 14 to 18 small red-skinned potatoes in 2 lbs (1 kg). Choose potatoes that are similar in size for even cooking and better presentation.

- Preheat barbecue grill to medium heat
- 6 sheets heavy-duty foil, sprayed with nonstick cooking spray

2 lbs	red-skinned potatoes, cut into ¼-inch (0.5 cm) slices	1 kg
2	cloves garlic, minced	2
1 tbsp	dried Italian seasoning	15 mL
2 tsp	kosher salt	10 mL
½ cup	ready-to-use chicken broth	125 mL
1 tbsp	virgin olive oil	15 mL
¼ cup	freshly grated Parmesan cheese	60 mL

1. In a large bowl, toss together potatoes, garlic, Italian seasoning, salt, broth and oil.

2. Fold edges of foil up into a bowl shape. Arrange potato mixture on prepared foil sheets, dividing evenly. Fold foil into tent-style packets and seal edges tightly.

3. Place packets on preheated grill and cook for 20 minutes, rotating a half-turn halfway through, until potatoes are just tender. Open packets with caution, allowing steam to escape, and loosely peel back foil. Sprinkle potatoes with Parmesan, dividing evenly. Cook, without resealing, for 5 minutes or until cheese is light golden.

Variation

Use ⅔ cup (150 mL) Italian dressing in place of the Italian seasoning, salt, broth and oil.

Spirited Hasselback Potatoes

Makes 6 servings

If you have ever finished all the delicious seasonings and buttery toppings before you're even halfway through eating a baked potato, you will be grateful for these spirited potatoes that are delicious from beginning to end.

Tip

To help you slice each potato without cutting through to the bottom, lay a chopstick on each side of the potato. The chopsticks will stop your knife before you cut through.

- Preheat barbecue grill to medium heat
- 6 sheets heavy-duty foil, sprayed with nonstick cooking spray

4	cloves garlic, minced	4
2 tsp	kosher salt	10 mL
3 tbsp	dried herbes de Provence	45 mL
½ cup	butter, melted	125 mL
6	large yellow-fleshed potatoes (each about 4 oz/125 g)	6
	Sour cream (optional)	

1. In a small bowl, combine garlic, salt, herbes de Provence and butter.

2. Without cutting all the way through to the bottom, cut potatoes crosswise into ¼-inch (0.5 cm) slices. Carefully open up the slices as much as possible without breaking off sections.

3. Place a potato on each prepared foil sheet. Brush butter mixture inside the potato slices and on top of the potatoes. Fold foil into tent-style packets and seal edges tightly.

4. Place packets on preheated grill and cook for 45 to 60 minutes, rotating a half-turn halfway, until potatoes are tender. If desired, serve dolloped with sour cream.

Bacon Ranch Potato Bundles

If you are looking for a quick and easy side dish with easy cleanup, these scrumptious potato packets are a must try.

Tip

If you prefer, these packets can be baked in a 350°F (180°C) oven for 25 to 30 minutes, rotating a half-turn halfway through, until potatoes are tender.

- Preheat barbecue grill to medium heat
- 4 sheets heavy-duty foil, sprayed with nonstick cooking spray

2 lbs	small red-skinned potatoes, thinly sliced (about 4 cups/1 L)	1 kg
8	slices bacon, cooked crisp and crumbled	8
1	packet (1 oz/28 g) dry ranch dressing mix	1
	Kosher salt and freshly ground black pepper	
¼ cup	butter, cut into pieces	60 mL
	Sour cream (optional)	
	Chopped fresh chives (optional)	

1. Arrange potatoes on prepared foil sheets, dividing evenly. Sprinkle with bacon and ranch dressing. Season with salt and pepper. Top with butter, dividing evenly. Fold foil into tent-style packets and seal edges tightly.

2. Place packets on preheated grill and cook for 20 to 25 minutes, rotating a half-turn halfway through, until potatoes are tender. If desired, serve dolloped with sour cream and sprinkled with chives.

Bacon and Cheese Steak Fries

Prepare this game-day favorite at your tailgate party or grill it at home — either way, you will love these hearty fries.

Tips

Use a baking sheet to help you transfer the packets to and from the grill.

If you have a hearty bunch to feed and are serving this with only a few other appetizers, you may want to allow for it to serve 4 to 6 people, instead of 8. The recipe is easily doubled if you want to make more.

- Preheat barbecue grill to medium heat
- 2 double sheets heavy-duty foil, top sheets sprayed with nonstick cooking spray

1	package (28 oz/796 g) frozen steak fries	1
1½ cups	shredded Cheddar cheese	375 mL
6	slices bacon, cooked crisp and crumbled	6
4	green onions, sliced	4

1. Divide fries evenly between prepared foil sheets. Fold foil into tent-style packets, leaving enough room to add the remaining ingredients later, and seal edges tightly.

2. Place packets on preheated grill, cover and cook for 10 minutes. Rotate packets a quarter-turn and open tops with caution, allowing steam to escape. Sprinkle fries with cheese, bacon and green onions, dividing evenly. Reseal packets and cook for 8 to 10 minutes or until fries are cooked through and cheese is melted.

Simply Fabulous Seasoned Sweet Vidalia Onion Blossoms

Makes 4 servings

Here's another game-day snacking favorite. These onion blossoms come out soft, caramelly and cheesy. What could be better? Pull off individual onion slices to eat.

Tips

To help you slice the onion without cutting through to the bottom, lay a chopstick on each side of the onion. The chopsticks will stop your knife before you cut through.

To test the onion for doneness, pull on an onion sliver. If it pulls away easily, the onion is ready to serve.

Serve with a horseradish dip or creamy chili dip.

The sauce recipe can easily be doubled, and you can store the extra sauce in the refrigerator for up to 1 week.

- Preheat barbecue grill to medium-high heat
- Double sheet heavy-duty foil, top sheet sprayed with nonstick cooking spray

½ cup	ketchup	125 mL
2 tsp	prepared yellow mustard	10 mL
2 tsp	Worcestershire sauce	10 mL
1½ tsp	apple cider vinegar	7 mL
1 drop	hot pepper sauce	1 drop
¼ tsp	salt	1 mL
¼ tsp	freshly ground black pepper	1 mL
1	large Vidalia onion	1
3 tbsp	shredded mozzarella cheese	45 mL

1. In a medium bowl, combine ketchup, mustard, Worcestershire sauce, vinegar, hot pepper sauce, salt and pepper.

2. Place onion root side down on cutting board. Without cutting all the way through to the bottom, cut onion into 6 wedges. Place on prepared foil sheet and gently spread onion layers apart in the wedges to form a "blossom." Sprinkle with cheese and drizzle with prepared sauce. Fold foil into a flat packet and seal edges tightly.

3. Place packet on preheated grill and cook for 35 to 40 minutes, rotating a quarter-turn occasionally, until onion is tender and lightly browned.

Sweet-and-Savory Red Onion Roast

These grilled onions are delicious on a pulled pork sandwich or as an accompaniment to grilled bratwurst, sausages or burgers. Serve alongside Cajun Grilled Onions and Peppers (page 129) as an alternative for guests who prefer a sweeter condiment.

Tips

Any jam you prefer can be used in place of the plum jam.

Three white or yellow onions would also work well in place of the red onions in this recipe.

Use a baking sheet to help you transfer the packet to and from the grill.

• Preheat barbecue grill to medium-high heat
• Double sheet heavy-duty foil, top sheet sprayed with nonstick cooking spray

2 tbsp	virgin olive oil	30 mL
1 tbsp	plum jam	15 mL
2 tsp	white vinegar	10 mL
2	red onions, thinly sliced crosswise and separated into rings	2
	Kosher salt and freshly ground black pepper	

1. In a small bowl, combine oil, jam and vinegar. Add onions and toss to coat.

2. Transfer onion mixture to prepared foil sheet. Season with salt and pepper. Fold foil into a tent-style packet and seal edges tightly.

3. Place packet on preheated grill and cook for 12 minutes, rotating a half-turn halfway through, until onions are tender.

Cajun Grilled Onions and Peppers

Cajun-seasoned grilled onions and peppers are a delectable accompaniment to grilled bratwurst, sausages, hot dogs and burgers. Guests can choose how spicy to make their entrée by adding more or less of this mixture on top.

Tip

You can purchase a prepared Cajun seasoning mix and use 1 tbsp (15 mL) in place of the blend prepared in step 1. What I like about making my own seasoning is that I can adjust the spice and other flavors to my liking.

- Preheat barbecue grill to medium-high heat
- 2 double sheets heavy-duty foil, top sheets sprayed with nonstick cooking spray

1 tsp	paprika	5 mL
¼ tsp	garlic powder	1 mL
¼ tsp	dried oregano	1 mL
¼ tsp	freshly ground black pepper	1 mL
¼ tsp	ground nutmeg	1 mL
½ tsp	Worcestershire sauce	2 mL
2 drops	hot pepper sauce	2 drops
2	large onions, cut crosswise into ¼-inch (0.5 cm) thick slices and rings separated	2
1	green bell pepper, thinly sliced	1
1	red bell pepper, thinly sliced	1
½ cup	butter, cut into small pieces	125 mL

1. In a small bowl, combine paprika, garlic powder, oregano, pepper, nutmeg, Worcestershire sauce and hot pepper sauce.

2. Divide onions, green pepper and red pepper evenly between prepared foil sheets. Dot evenly with butter. Drizzle seasoning mixture over vegetables. Fold foil into tent-style packets and seal edges tightly.

3. Place packets on preheated grill and cook for 8 minutes, turning packets over once. Reduce heat to low and cook for 10 minutes or until vegetables are tender.

Zesty Vegetables and Portobello Mushrooms

The fresh Mediterranean-influenced ingredients in this recipe make for a mouthwatering and uniquely satisfying side dish.

Tip

This dish makes a wonderful accompaniment to grilled lamb chops or beef kabobs.

- Preheat barbecue grill to medium heat
- 2 double sheets heavy-duty foil, top sheets sprayed with nonstick cooking spray

4	canned artichoke hearts, drained and quartered	4
2	portobello mushrooms, stemmed and quartered	2
1	small bulb fennel, quartered	1
1	zucchini, cut into 1-inch (2.5 cm) pieces	1
¼ cup	virgin olive oil	60 mL
	Kosher salt and freshly ground pepper	
1 tbsp	fresh rosemary leaves	15 mL
½ cup	sun-dried tomato vinaigrette	125 mL

1. Divide artichokes, mushrooms, fennel and zucchini between prepared foil sheets. Brush with oil, coating well. Season with salt and pepper. Sprinkle with rosemary. Fold foil into tent-style packets and seal edges tightly.

2. Place packets on preheated grill, cover and cook for 15 to 20 minutes, rotating a quarter-turn occasionally, until vegetables are tender. Transfer vegetables to a serving platter and drizzle with vinaigrette.

Italian-Seasoned Summer Vegetables, Mushrooms and Red Onions

Makes 4 servings

This is the perfect complementary side dish for grilled steak, chicken, lamb or pork.

Tip

For ease in transferring the packets to the grill, place them on a rimless baking sheet and slide them off the baking sheet onto the grill.

- Preheat barbecue grill to medium-high heat
- 2 double sheets heavy-duty foil, top sheets sprayed with nonstick cooking spray

8	mushrooms	8
3	cloves garlic, minced	3
2	small tomatoes, cut into ¼-inch (0.5 cm) thick slices	2
1	red bell pepper, cut into strips	1
1	zucchini, thinly sliced	1
1	red onion, thinly sliced	1
1 tsp	dried basil	5 mL
1 tsp	seasoning salt	5 mL
3 tbsp	virgin olive oil	45 mL
3 tbsp	freshly squeezed lemon juice	45 mL
	Hot pepper flakes (optional)	
¼ cup	freshly grated Parmesan cheese (optional)	60 mL

1. In a large bowl, toss together mushrooms, garlic, tomatoes, red pepper, zucchini, onion, basil, seasoning salt, oil and lemon juice.

2. Divide vegetable mixture evenly among prepared foil sheets. Fold foil into tent-style packets and seal edges tightly.

3. Place packets on preheated grill and cook for 10 to 12 minutes or until vegetables are tender-crisp. If desired, serve sprinkled with hot pepper flakes and Parmesan.

Fiery Fava Bean and Sweet Corn Succotash

This dish originated during the Great Depression in the United States. As often happens, out of necessity, we create a flavorful dish that we want to make again and again.

Tip

If you want to use fresh ingredients, you will need about 3 cups (750 mL) shelled fava beans and about 4 medium ears of corn, shucked, in place of frozen.

- Preheat barbecue grill to medium heat
- 6 sheets heavy-duty foil, sprayed with nonstick cooking spray

1	package (28 oz/796 g) frozen fava beans	1
1	package (28 oz/796 g) frozen corn kernels	1
1	tomato, chopped	1
2	cloves garlic, minced	2
¼ tsp	hot pepper flakes	1 mL
2 tbsp	butter, melted	30 mL
	Salt and freshly ground black pepper	
¼ cup	chopped fresh basil	60 mL

1. In a large bowl, combine beans, corn and tomato. Stir in garlic, hot pepper flakes and butter. Season to taste with salt and pepper.

2. Divide bean mixture evenly among prepared foil sheets. Fold foil into tent-style packets and seal edges tightly.

3. Place packets on preheated grill and cook for 15 to 18 minutes, rotating a half-turn halfway through, until vegetables are heated through and tender. Serve sprinkled with basil.

Grilled Banana Splits

An old-time favorite gets a new twist with gooey caramelized bananas. Topped with vanilla ice cream, this dessert will always be a favorite.

Tip

Use a small paring knife or the tip of a spoon to cut the groove in the banana. You can nibble on the cut-out banana or add it as a topping along with the ice cream.

- Preheat barbecue grill to medium heat
- 4 sheets heavy-duty foil, sprayed with nonstick cooking spray

4	bananas (peel intact)	4
2 cups	mini marshmallows	500 mL
4 tbsp	chocolate chips	60 mL
4	scoops vanilla ice cream	4

1. Peel back one section of each banana, leaving peel attached. Cut a small groove down the length of the banana. Pack marshmallows and chocolate chips into the groove. Replace banana peel over the fillings.

2. Place each stuffed banana on a prepared foil sheet. Fold foil into flat packets and seal edges tightly.

3. Place packets on preheated grill and cook for 5 minutes or until fillings are melted. Serve each portion with a scoop of ice cream.

Variation

For a supersized banana split, top the cooked bananas with strawberry jam, crushed pineapple and chopped nuts before adding the ice cream.

Crazy Apple Crunch

If you have a serious sweet tooth, this sweet and crunchy apple dessert will make you squeal with delight.

Tip

Use a baking sheet to help you transfer the packets to and from the grill.

- Preheat barbecue grill to medium heat
- 4 sheets heavy-duty foil, sprayed with nonstick cooking spray

4	apples (such as Granny Smith or Honeygold), peeled and chopped	4
1 cup	raisins	250 mL
½ cup	granola	125 mL
1½ tbsp	butter, cut into small pieces	22 mL
12	large marshmallows	12
¼ cup	pure maple syrup or liquid honey	60 mL

1. Divide apples, raisins and granola evenly among prepared foil sheets. Dot apples with butter. Top with marshmallows and drizzle with maple syrup, dividing evenly. Fold foil into tent-style packets and seal edges tightly.

2. Place packets on preheated grill and cook for 10 minutes or until apples are softened and marshmallows are melted.

Variation

Substitute chopped nuts, such as walnuts or pecans, for the granola.

Blackberry Peach Crumble

When beautiful berries are ripe for the taking and chin-dripping peaches are calling you at the market, it is the perfect time to make this decadent dessert.

Tips

If your blackberries are very large, you may want to cut them in half or crush them slightly.

- Preheat barbecue grill to medium heat
- 4 sheets heavy-duty foil, sprayed with nonstick cooking spray

3	peaches, peeled and thinly sliced	3
2 cups	blackberries	500 mL
2 tbsp	freshly squeezed lemon juice	30 mL
1 tsp	vanilla extract	5 mL
2 tbsp	granulated sugar	30 mL
1/3 cup	all-purpose flour	75 mL
1/4 cup	large-flake (old-fashioned) rolled oats	60 mL
1 tbsp	packed brown sugar	15 mL
1/2 tsp	ground cinnamon	2 mL
2 tbsp	cold unsalted butter, cut into small pieces	30 mL

1. In a large bowl, combine peaches, blackberries, lemon juice and vanilla. Sprinkle with granulated sugar and gently toss to coat. Let stand for 15 minutes.

2. Meanwhile, in a medium bowl, combine flour, oats, brown sugar and cinnamon. Using a pastry blender or fork, cut in butter until crumbly.

3. Fold up the sides of each prepared foil sheet, creating a bowl shape. Divide blackberry mixture among packets, dividing evenly. Sprinkle evenly with crumb mixture. Fold foil into tent-style packets and seal edges tightly.

4. Place packets on preheated grill and cook for 15 minutes. Open packets with caution, allowing steam to escape, and cook for 3 to 4 minutes or until crumble mixture is golden brown and peaches are softened.

Variation

For the best results, keep your butter cold until cutting it into the crumb mixture.

Substitute 4 plums, thinly sliced, for the peaches.

Oven Recipes

Pork, Beef and Lamb

Side Dishes

Desserts

Spicy Glazed Snack-Time Nuts

Makes 4 servings		

A perfect snack for game day or happy hour, these nuts are packed with a sweet and spicy punch.

Tip

Pecan halves and peanuts are nice alternatives to the mixed nuts. When using pecans or unsalted peanuts, add 1 tsp (5 mL) salt in step 1.

- Preheat oven to 375°F (190°C)
- Double sheet heavy-duty foil, top sheet sprayed with nonstick cooking spray

2 cups	salted mixed nuts	500 mL
2 tsp	granulated sugar	10 mL
1 tsp	chipotle chile powder	5 mL
¼ tsp	ground cumin	1 mL
¼ tsp	freshly ground black pepper	1 mL
1 tbsp	butter, cut into small pieces	15 mL

1. In a medium bowl, toss together nuts, sugar, chipotle powder, cumin, pepper and butter.

2. Place nut mixture in center of prepared foil sheet. Fold foil into a flat packet and seal edges tightly. Place packet on a baking sheet.

3. Bake in preheated oven for 15 to 18 minutes, turning packet over two to three times, until nuts are nicely coated. Remove from oven and open packet with caution, allowing steam to escape. Spread nuts out on foil to cool.

Jalapeño and Jack–Topped French Bread

In this easy alternative to jalapeño poppers, the jalapeños and gooey cheese are paired with crusty French bread.

Tip

If you have a longer French bread loaf, cut it in half crosswise, then horizontally. Use a total of 4 double sheets heavy-duty foil, top sheets sprayed with nonstick cooking spray. Divide the cut loaf quarters among the 4 prepared sheets.

- Preheat oven 350°F (180°C)
- 2 double sheets heavy-duty foil, top sheets sprayed with nonstick cooking spray

1 lb	Monterey Jack cheese, shredded	500 g
2 tbsp	mayonnaise	30 mL
1	loaf French bread (about 1 lb/500 g), cut in half horizontally	1
1 tbsp	butter, softened	15 mL
⅔ cup	sliced jalapeño peppers	150 mL

1. In a small bowl, combine cheese and mayonnaise.

2. Place bread, cut side up, on prepared foil sheets. Spread butter on cut sides of bread. Arrange jalapeños evenly over top. Spread cheese mixture over jalapeños. Fold foil into tent-style packets and seal edges tightly. Place packets on a baking sheet.

3. Bake in preheated oven for 20 to 25 minutes or until cheese is melted and light golden brown. Remove from oven and open packets with caution, allowing steam to escape. Let cool for 5 minutes before cutting into slices.

Bacon-Wrapped Sea Scallops with Dijon Mustard

Makes 12 servings

For the perfect appetizer, make these Dijon-enhanced scallops wrapped in savory bacon and watch them disappear right before your eyes.

Tip

If you like your bacon crispier, you can cook it first, in a skillet over medium heat, for 5 to 7 minutes or until just softened. The bacon needs to remain soft so that it will easily wrap around the scallops.

- Preheat oven to 450°F (230°C)
- Triple sheet heavy-duty foil, top sheet sprayed with nonstick cooking spray
- Rimmed baking sheet
- Toothpicks

2 tbsp	liquid honey	30 mL
2 tbsp	Dijon mustard	30 mL
2 tbsp	virgin olive oil	30 mL
1 tbsp	white vinegar	15 mL
1 lb	scallops (24 to 30 count), side muscles removed	500 g
8 oz	thick-cut bacon slices, cut in half	250 g

1. In a medium bowl, combine honey, mustard, oil and vinegar. Dip scallops and bacon in mixture. Wrap a piece of bacon around each scallop.

2. Place bacon-wrapped scallops on prepared foil sheet. Fold foil into a flat packet and seal edges tightly. Place packet on baking sheet.

3. Bake in preheated oven for 12 to 15 minutes or until bacon is slightly crispy and scallops are firm and opaque. Remove from oven and open packets with caution, allowing steam to escape. Skewer wraps with toothpicks to serve.

Zesty Herb Party Wings

|||||||||||||||||||||||||||||||||||||||||||||||||||||||||||||||||||||||||||||||||||||||||||||||||||||||||||||||||||||||||||||||||||

These wings are the
perfect trio of sweet,
tangy and zesty —
a fun addition to
an appetizer party
or a flavorful game
day snack. They are
marinated ahead of
time so you can just
pop them in the oven a
half-hour before you're
ready to serve.

Tip

If this is the only dish or one
of a few dishes you will be
serving, allow for 6 wing
sections per person. If you
are serving more appetizers
or snacks, allow for 3 wing
sections per person.

- 13- by 9-inch (33 by 23 cm) glass baking dish
- 3 double sheets heavy-duty foil, top sheets sprayed with nonstick cooking spray

4	green onions (white and green parts), finely chopped	4
2	cloves garlic, minced	2
¼ cup	packed dark brown sugar	60 mL
1 tbsp	prepared horseradish	15 mL
1 cup	hoisin sauce	250 mL
½ cup	unsweetened pomegranate juice	125 mL
3 tbsp	vegetable oil	45 mL
	Freshly ground black pepper	
18	chicken wings, sections split apart, wing tips reserved or discarded	18
½ cup	french-fried onions, crushed	125 mL

1. In a medium saucepan, combine green onions, garlic, brown sugar, horseradish, hoisin sauce, pomegranate juice and oil. Season to taste with pepper. Bring to a boil over medium-high heat, stirring constantly. Reduce heat and simmer, stirring occasionally, for 20 minutes or until sauce is thickened.

2. Spread wings out evenly in bottom of baking dish and season with salt. Pour sauce over wings and toss to coat. Cover with plastic wrap and refrigerate for at least 1 hour or up to 2 hours before baking.

3. Preheat oven to 375°F (190°C).

4. Divide wings evenly among prepared foil sheets. Drizzle evenly with marinade. Fold foil into flat packets and seal edges tightly. Place packets on a baking sheet.

5. Bake for 25 minutes, turning packets over once, until juices run clear when chicken is pierced. Serve sprinkled with crushed onions.

Half-Time Brown Sugar Mustard Ham Rolls

These ham and Swiss cheese sandwiches are bursting with flavor from a sautéed mustard and onion spread. They're great for parties or as the perfect comfort-food sandwich.

Tips

The baked sandwiches can also be quartered if you want to serve them as demi-sandwiches along with more appetizers or snacks. In that case, you will have 24 servings.

Pretzel rolls are a great alternative to the kaiser rolls.

- Preheat oven to 350°F (180°C)
- 6 double sheets heavy-duty foil, top sheets sprayed with nonstick cooking spray

⅓ cup	butter	75 mL
½ cup	chopped onion	125 mL
1 tbsp	packed brown sugar	15 mL
1 tsp	dry mustard	5 mL
1 tsp	poppy seeds	5 mL
1 tsp	Worcestershire sauce	5 mL
6	medium kaiser rolls, split in half	6
12 oz	sliced deli ham	375 g
6 oz	Swiss cheese, shredded	175 g

1. In a medium saucepan, melt butter over medium heat. Add onion, brown sugar, mustard, poppy seeds and Worcestershire sauce; cook, stirring, until onion is translucent and sauce is thickened.

2. Place the bottom half of each roll, split side up, on a prepared foil sheet and spread roll with sauce. Divide ham and cheese evenly among rolls. Cover with top halves of rolls. Fold foil into flat packets and seal edges tightly. Place packets on a baking sheet.

3. Bake in preheated oven for 20 minutes or until cheese is melted and sandwiches are heated through. Remove from oven and open packets with caution, allowing steam to escape. Let stand for 5 minutes. Cut sandwiches in half to serve.

Easy Three-Cheese Spinach Lasagna

Always a favorite, this lasagna has the perfect blend of cheeses, spinach and sauce. With no-boil noodles, easy assembly and no mess to clean up, you can't go wrong.

Tips

If you are able to find pan liners that are foil on one side and parchment on the other, these work very well for the top sheets. Make sure to still add two layers of heavy-duty foil under each pan liner.

The ricotta filling can be prepared up to 1 day in advance and refrigerated. Let filling come to room temperature for up to 30 minutes or add 5 minutes to the baking time before opening the foil.

The leftover egg whites can be stored in an airtight container in the refrigerator for up to 2 days before use.

- Preheat oven to 375°F (190°C), with rack placed in upper third
- Food processor
- 3 triple sheets heavy-duty foil
- 3 sheets parchment paper

2	containers (each 15 oz/475 g) ricotta cheese	1
2	large egg yolks	2
1½ cups	packed basil leaves	375 mL
½ cup	freshly grated Parmesan cheese	125 mL
1½ tsp	kosher salt, divided	7 mL
¼ tsp	freshly ground black pepper	1 mL
2	packages (each 10 oz/300 g) frozen chopped spinach, thawed and squeezed dry	2
3¼ cups	tomato pasta sauce	800 mL
9	no-boil (oven-ready) lasagna noodles	9
4 cups	shredded mozzarella cheese	1 L

1. In food processor, combine ricotta, egg yolks, basil, Parmesan, 1 tsp (5 mL) salt and pepper; process until well blended.

2. In a medium bowl, toss spinach with the remaining salt.

3. Place a sheet of parchment paper on top of each prepared foil sheet. Fold up edges of each sheet to form a rectangular bowl slightly larger than 1 lasagna noodle. Add ⅔ cup (150 mL) pasta sauce to each "bowl," followed by 1 lasagna noodle, ½ cup (125 mL) ricotta mixture, one-ninth of the spinach and 2 tbsp (30 mL) mozzarella. Repeat layers twice more, without adding mozzarella to the last layer. Top with the remaining pasta sauce and sprinkle with the remaining mozzarella, dividing evenly. Fold foil into tent-style packets and seal edges tightly. Place packets on a baking sheet.

4. Bake in preheated oven for 45 minutes. Open the tops of the foil packets and bake for 20 minutes or until tops are lightly browned and bubbly. Let stand for 10 minutes before cutting and serving.

Corn- and Quinoa-Stuffed Red Peppers

These filling and delectable stuffed bell peppers make a hearty vegetarian entrée or are a wonderful side to any main dish.

Tips

You can substitute ¾ cup (175 mL) thawed frozen corn for the canned corn.

For 3 cups (750 mL) cooked quinoa, you'll need about ¾ cup (175 mL) raw. Cook according to package directions.

- Preheat oven to 350°F (180°C)
- 6 double sheets heavy-duty foil, top sheets sprayed with nonstick cooking spray

1 tbsp	virgin olive oil	15 mL
1	red onion, chopped	1
8 oz	mushrooms, sliced	250 g
7	large red bell peppers	7
1	can (10 oz/284 mL) corn kernels, drained	1
½ cup	chopped fresh parsley	125 mL
4 oz	baby spinach	125 g
3 cups	cooked quinoa	750 mL
1½ tsp	ground cinnamon	7 mL
1 tsp	ground cumin	5 mL
	Kosher salt and freshly ground black pepper	
½ cup	roasted cashew pieces	125 mL

1. In a large skillet, heat oil over medium heat. Add onion and cook, stirring, for 5 to 7 minutes or until translucent. Add mushrooms and cook, stirring, for 7 to 9 minutes or until softened and moisture has evaporated.

2. Meanwhile, chop 1 red pepper. Add chopped pepper, corn, parsley and spinach to skillet and cook, stirring, for 3 to 5 minutes or until spinach is wilted. Add quinoa, cinnamon and cumin, tossing gently to combine. Season to taste with salt and pepper. Add cashews and cook, stirring, for 2 minutes or until well combined.

3. Cut off and reserve the tops of the remaining red peppers. Core the peppers and remove the seeds. Place a pepper on each prepared foil sheet. Divide quinoa mixture evenly among peppers, packing mixture to fully fill each pepper. Top each pepper with the reserved top (the tops do not need to close the peppers). Fold foil up around peppers and seal edges tightly, being careful not to let stems pierce the foil. Place packets on a baking sheet.

4. Bake in preheated oven for 1 hour or until peppers are tender and filling is heated through.

Mediterranean Marinated Skirt Steak
and Vegetables (page 114)

Grilled Lamb and Vegetables
with Cucumber Yogurt Sauce (page 120)

Blackberry Peach Crumble (page 135)

Loaded Baked
Sweet Potatoes (page 145)

Coconut Lime Shrimp with Plantains
and Mango Salsa (page 157)

Curry Coconut Chicken with
Zucchini and Carrots (page 164)

Hoisin-Glazed Country-Style Ribs with
Green Beans and Crispy Leeks (page 171)

Herb-Crusted Sirloin Tip Roast
with Rosemary Beets (page 182)

Loaded Baked Sweet Potatoes

Makes 6 servings

Roasted sweet potatoes are elevated to a new flavor level with black beans, peppers and onions, creating a hearty vegetarian meal that even meat lovers will enjoy.

Tip

Sweet potato skins can be eaten, if desired. Choose sweet potatoes that do not have a waxy or dyed exterior. Organically grown or farmers' market sweet potatoes are your best choice for this.

- Preheat oven to 400°F (200°C)
- 6 sheets heavy-duty foil, sprayed with nonstick cooking spray

6	sweet potatoes (each about 5 oz/150 g)	6
1 tsp	virgin olive oil	5 mL
1	can (14 to 19 oz/398 to 540 mL) black beans, rinsed and drained	1
1	red bell pepper, finely chopped	1
1	small red onion, finely chopped	1
1 tsp	chili powder	5 mL
1 tsp	paprika	5 mL
	Kosher salt	
½ cup	plain Greek yogurt	125 mL
1 tsp	taco seasoning	5 mL
½ cup	salsa	125 mL
½ cup	shredded Mexican cheese blend	125 mL
¼ cup	chopped green onions	60 mL

1. Brush skin of sweet potatoes with oil. Place a sweet potato on each prepared foil sheet. Prick tops of sweet potatoes with a fork. Wrap foil tightly around sweet potatoes. Bake in preheated oven for 20 minutes or until slightly softened.

2. Meanwhile, in a medium bowl, combine beans, red pepper, onion, chili powder and paprika. Season to taste with salt.

3. Carefully, to avoid tearing foil, open packets and cut a large slice across the top of each sweet potato. Lightly mash sweet potato flesh with a fork. Pack bean mixture into sweet potatoes, dividing evenly. Fold foil into tent-style packets and seal edges tightly. Place packets on a baking sheet.

4. Bake for 15 to 20 minutes or until sweet potatoes are softened to your liking and toppings are heated through.

5. Meanwhile, in a small bowl, combine yogurt and taco seasoning.

6. Serve sweet potatoes topped with seasoned yogurt, salsa, cheese and green onions.

Ginger Soy Eggplant and Tofu Bundles

Here, tofu and eggplant are marinated in a ginger garlic sauce that infuses them with flavor. They are ideal served over rice or cucumbers, or can be skewered as an appetizer.

Tip

This dish is wonderful over a cucumber and citrus salad or cooked long-grain rice.

• 4 double sheets heavy-duty foil, top sheets sprayed with nonstick cooking spray

20 oz	firm tofu, cut into 16 cubes	600 g
2	green onions, chopped	2
1	medium eggplant, cut into chunks	1
2 tbsp	minced gingerroot	30 mL
2 tbsp	minced garlic	30 mL
¼ cup	soy sauce or tamari	60 mL
¼ cup	grapeseed oil	60 mL

1. In a large sealable plastic bag, combine tofu, green onions, eggplant, ginger, garlic, soy sauce and oil. Seal bag and turn to coat all ingredients. Refrigerate for at least 2 hours or up to 24 hours.

2. Preheat oven to 400°F (200°C).

3. Divide tofu mixture evenly among prepared foil sheets. Fold foil into flat packets and seal edges tightly. Place packets on a baking sheet.

4. Bake for 10 minutes, turning packets over once, until eggplant is tender.

Mediterranean Haddock with Olives

Cherry tomatoes, black olives and white wine coalesce into a delicious sauce that enhances the delicate haddock in this Mediterranean-inspired dish. Serve with steamed French-cut green beans for a light and soothing meal.

Tips

Pull the fine fennel fronds from the stalk to use as garnish. They can be chopped if you prefer. Any remaining fronds can be stored in a sealable plastic bag in the refrigerator for up to 5 days. They are wonderful in salads, particularly potato salads, in pesto or as a garnish for soups.

Halibut or cod are good substitutions for the haddock. For thicker fillets, such as halibut, increase the baking time to 22 to 28 minutes.

You can substitute ready-to-use vegetable broth for the wine, if you prefer.

- Preheat oven to 400°F (200°C)
- 2 double sheets heavy-duty foil, top sheets sprayed with nonstick cooking spray

10	cherry tomatoes, halved	10
1	bulb fennel, fronds reserved (see tip, at left) and bulb julienned	1
1	lemon, thinly sliced	1
2 tbsp	pitted black olives	30 mL
2 tbsp	virgin olive oil	30 mL
2	skinless haddock fillets (each about 4 oz/125 g)	2
	Freshly ground black pepper	
¼ cup	dry white wine	60 mL

1. In a large bowl, toss together tomatoes, julienned fennel, lemon, olives and oil.

2. Place a haddock fillet on each prepared foil sheet. Fold edges of foil up into a bowl shape around the fish. Season with pepper. Top fish with tomato mixture, dividing evenly. Drizzle evenly with wine and garnish with fennel fronds. Fold foil into tent-style packets and seal edges tightly. Place packets on a baking sheet.

3. Bake in preheated oven for 18 to 22 minutes or until fish is opaque and flakes evenly when tested with a fork.

Parmesan-Crusted Halibut with Roasted Root Vegetables

IIIIIIIIIIIIIIIIIIIIIIIIIIIIIIIIIIIIIIIIIIIIIIIIIIIIIIIIIIIIIIIIIIIIIIIIIIIIIIIIIIIIIIIIIIIIIIIIIIIIIIIIIIIIIIIIIIIIIIIIIIIIIIIIIIIIIIIIIIIIIIII

Makes 6 servings

If you like spicy food, you will want to dive right in to this Parmesan-crusted halibut with a side of roasted carrots and parsnips. The infusion of flavors and the incredibly moist fish make this a memorable dish.

Tip

Cod or haddock make an equally satisfying and sometimes less expensive replacement for the halibut. Reduce the cooking time to 18 to 22 minutes for these thinner fillets.

- Preheat oven to 400°F (200°C)
- Triple sheet heavy-duty foil, top sheet sprayed with nonstick cooking spray

1½ lb	skinless halibut fillet	750 g
2	carrots, thinly sliced lengthwise	2
2	parsnips, thinly sliced lengthwise	2
¼ cup	virgin olive oil, divided	60 mL
	Kosher salt and freshly ground black pepper	
1½ tsp	freshly squeezed lemon juice	7 mL
¼ cup	butter	60 mL
2 tbsp	minced garlic	30 mL
1 tbsp	chopped fresh thyme	15 mL
½ tsp	hot pepper flakes	2 mL
3	green onions, sliced	3
½ cup	freshly grated Parmesan cheese	125 mL
½ tsp	paprika	2 mL
3 tbsp	mayonnaise	45 mL
1 tsp	Sriracha or other hot pepper sauce	5 mL

1. Place prepared foil sheet on a baking sheet. Place halibut fillet in center of foil. Arrange carrots and parsnips around fish. Drizzle vegetables with oil. Season fish and vegetables with salt and black pepper. Drizzle fish with lemon juice. Fold foil into a flat packet and seal edges tightly.

2. Bake in preheated oven for 20 to 25 minutes or until fish is opaque and flakes easily when tested with a fork.

3. Meanwhile, in a small skillet, melt butter over medium heat. Add garlic, thyme and hot pepper flakes; cook, stirring, for 2 to 3 minutes or until fragrant.

4. In a small bowl, combine garlic mixture, green onions, Parmesan, paprika, ¼ tsp (1 mL) salt, ¼ tsp (1 mL) black pepper, mayonnaise and hot pepper sauce.

5. Remove baking sheet from oven and preheat broiler. Open packet with caution, allowing steam to escape, and spread Parmesan mixture evenly over fish.

6. Broil for 1 to 2 minutes or until fish is lightly browned and coating is bubbly.

Herbes de Provence Baked Salmon

This delicately seasoned baked salmon is fit for a king or queen — so simple, delicate and irresistible, you can almost hear the trumpets blaring for dinnertime.

Tip

This dish is wonderful with a side of roasted asparagus. Place 16 spears of trimmed asparagus on a sheet of heavy-duty foil. Drizzle with olive oil and season with kosher salt, tossing to coat. (Do not fold the foil into a packet for this one; just leave it open.) Add to the baking sheet, next to the salmon packets, for the last 15 minutes of baking time.

- Preheat oven to 350°F (180°C)
- 4 sheets heavy-duty foil, sprayed with nonstick cooking spray

1 lb	skin-on salmon fillet, cut into 4 pieces	500 g
3 tbsp	butter, melted	45 mL
	Kosher salt	
	Dried herbes de Provence	
3½ cups	cooked rice pilaf	875 mL

1. Place a piece of salmon, skin side down, on each prepared foil sheet. Brush top of salmon with butter and season with salt and herbes de Provence. Arrange rice around salmon, dividing evenly. Fold foil into a tent-style packet and seal edges tightly. Place packet on a baking sheet.

2. Bake in preheated oven for 25 to 30 minutes or until fish is opaque and flakes easily when tested with a fork.

Chili Salmon with Pineapple and Peppers

IIIIIIIIIIIIIIIIIIIIIIIIIIIIIIIIIIIIIIIIIIIIIIIIIIIIIIIIIIIIIIIIIIIIIIIIIIIIIIIIIIIIIIIIIIIIIIIIIIIIIIIIIIIIIIIIIIIIIIIIIIIIIIIIIIIIIIIIIIIIIIIIIIIIIIIII

Makes 4 servings

This salmon dish perks up all of your taste buds with a combination of savory, salty, spicy, fruity and sweet. Serve it over rice, and you have a truly sensational meal.

Tip

A sweet onion is the best choice for this recipe. A Walla Walla onion is a good substitute for the Vidalia.

- Preheat oven to 350°F (180°C)
- 4 double sheets heavy-duty foil, top sheets sprayed with nonstick cooking spray

1 cup	canned crushed pineapple	250 mL
½ cup	dry white wine	125 mL
1 tsp	minced gingerroot	5 mL
1 tsp	sesame oil	5 mL
1 tbsp	teriyaki glaze	15 mL
2 tbsp	virgin coconut oil, melted	30 mL
1	red bell pepper, cut into strips	1
1	green bell pepper, cut into strips	1
1	Vidalia onion, cut in half and sliced	1
1 lb	skin-on salmon fillet, cut into 4 pieces	500 g
2 tsp	kosher salt	10 mL
1 tsp	chipotle chile powder	5 mL

1. In a medium bowl, combine pineapple, wine, ginger, oil and teriyaki glaze.

2. Fold each prepared foil sheet into a bowl shape. Divide coconut oil evenly among sheets. Arrange red pepper, green pepper and onion on top, dividing evenly. Place salmon, skin side up, on top of each mound of vegetables. Sprinkle fish with salt and chile powder. Pour pineapple mixture over fish, dividing evenly. Fold foil into flat packets and seal edges tightly. Place packets, fold side up, on a baking sheet.

3. Bake in preheated oven for 25 to 30 minutes, rotating packets a half-turn halfway through, until fish is opaque and flakes easily when tested with a fork.

Shanghai Sesame Swordfish and Peapods

Makes 4 servings

You will love the spicy and savory flavors of marinated swordfish, exquisitely presented on skewers with snow peas, cherry tomatoes and sesame seeds.

Tip

Toast sesame seeds in a small skillet over medium-high heat, shaking pan constantly, for 3 to 5 minutes or until light golden brown and fragrant. Watch closely to prevent burning.

- Preheat oven to 500°F (260°C)
- Triple sheet heavy-duty foil, top sheet sprayed with nonstick cooking spray
- Twelve 8-inch (20 cm) wooden skewers

2 tbsp	minced gingerroot	30 mL
2 tsp	Chinese five-spice powder	10 mL
¼ cup	soy sauce	60 mL
¼ cup	dry sherry	60 mL
2 tbsp	chile oil	30 mL
2 tsp	toasted sesame oil	10 mL
1 lb	swordfish steaks, cut into 1-inch (2.5 cm) cubes	500 g
8 oz	snow peas, trimmed	250 g
8 oz	cherry tomatoes	250 g
¼ cup	sesame seeds, toasted (see tip, at left)	60 mL

1. In a medium bowl, combine ginger, five-spice powder, soy sauce, sherry, chile oil and sesame oil. Transfer ⅓ cup (75 mL) marinade to a separate small bowl. Add swordfish to medium bowl and toss to coat.

2. Place prepared foil sheet on a baking sheet. Arrange marinated swordfish in center of foil. Fold foil into a flat packet and seal edges tightly.

3. Bake in preheated oven for 7 to 9 minutes or until fish is opaque and lightly browned.

4. Meanwhile, in a saucepan of boiling water, blanch snow peas for 1 minute. Drain and blot dry with a paper towel.

5. Dip one side of each swordfish cube in sesame seeds. Thread a tomato, then a snow pea, then a swordfish cube, coated side up, onto each skewer. Place skewers on a platter. Serve with the remaining Shanghai sauce for dipping.

Florentine Rainbow Trout with Wild Rice Pilaf

||||||||||||||||||||||||||||||||||||||||||||||||||||||||||||||||||||||||||||||||||||||||||||||||||||||||||||||||

Delicate rainbow trout gets a spectacular lift with spinach, garlic, shallots and pine nuts, for a savory meal with a hint of crunch.

Tip

In place of the fresh spinach, you can use a 12-oz (375 g) package of frozen spinach, thawed and squeezed dry.

- Preheat oven to 425°F (220°C)
- 4 double sheets heavy-duty foil, top sheets sprayed with nonstick cooking spray

1 lb	trimmed spinach leaves	500 g
	Water	
	Grated zest and juice of ½ lemon	
⅓ cup	butter	75 mL
3	cloves garlic, thinly sliced	3
1	shallot, thinly sliced	1
4	skin-on trout fillets (each about 6 oz/175 g)	4
	Kosher salt and freshly ground black pepper	
¼ cup	pine nuts	60 mL
2 cups	cooked wild rice pilaf	500 mL

1. In a large skillet, heat 2 tbsp (30 mL) water over medium heat. Working in batches, cook spinach until just wilted, adding more water as needed. Transfer to a colander and let cool. Press out excess liquid and chop. Transfer to a bowl and toss with lemon zest.

2. Meanwhile, in a small skillet, melt butter over medium heat. Cook until butter starts to brown. Add garlic and shallot; cook, stirring, for 1 minute or until just tender. Remove from heat and stir in lemon juice.

3. Add one-eighth of the garlic mixture to each prepared foil sheet. Arrange spinach on top, dividing evenly. Place a trout fillet, skin side down, on top of each mound of spinach and season with salt and pepper. Top with the remaining garlic mixture, dividing evenly. Sprinkle with pine nuts. Arrange wild rice pilaf around fish, dividing evenly. Fold foil into flat packets and seal edges tightly. Place packets on a baking sheet.

4. Bake in preheated oven for 10 to 12 minutes or until fish is opaque and flakes easily when tested with a fork.

Miso Tuna and Mushrooms

|||||||||||||||||||||||||||||||||||||||||||||||||||||||||||||||||||||||||||||||||||||||||||||||||||||||||||||||||||||||||||||

Makes 4 servings

Miso, mirin and ginger add flavor and richness to tuna and shiitake mushrooms, for a light and satisfying Japanese-inspired meal.

Tips

Cremini mushrooms can be substituted for the shiitakes.

If your tuna steak is more than 1 inch (2.5 cm) thick, increase the baking time by 3 to 5 minutes.

- Preheat oven to 425°F (220°C)
- 4 double sheets heavy-duty foil, top sheets sprayed with nonstick cooking spray

2 tsp	white or yellow miso	10 mL
1½ tbsp	mirin	22 mL
1 cup	sliced shiitake mushroom caps	250 mL
1 tsp	grated gingerroot	5 mL
1 lb	tuna steak, cut into 4 pieces	500 g
	Toasted sesame oil	
	Kosher salt and freshly ground black pepper	
2	green onions, thinly sliced	2

1. In a small bowl, combine miso and mirin.

2. Divide mushrooms and ginger evenly among prepared foil sheets. Place a tuna steak on top of each mound of mushrooms. Drizzle with oil and season with salt and pepper. Drizzle with miso mixture and sprinkle with green onions. Fold foil into tent-style packets and seal edges tightly. Place packets on a baking sheet.

3. Bake in preheated oven for 14 to 16 minutes or until fish is opaque and flakes easily when tested with a fork (or to desired doneness).

Thai Chili Tuna Medley

Makes 4 servings

Here, the simplicity of the preparation is surpassed only by the simplicity of the presentation: a Thai-inspired tuna medley nestled into lettuce leaf wraps. But the deep and spicy flavors remain unsurpassed.

Tips

Add the honey if you want to tone down the spice or like your dish a bit sweeter.

If you like spice, you can sprinkle the tuna mixture with Thai chile flakes before serving.

Bibb lettuce is also known as butter lettuce or Boston lettuce. Iceberg lettuce is a good alternative.

- Preheat oven to 350°F (180°C)
- 4 double sheets heavy-duty foil, top sheets sprayed with nonstick cooking spray

2	cloves garlic, minced	2
1	small onion, finely chopped	1
2 tsp	minced gingerroot	10 mL
¼ cup	sweet Thai chili sauce	60 mL
1 tbsp	soy sauce	15 mL
1 tbsp	sesame oil	15 mL
1 tsp	liquid honey (optional)	5 mL
2	cans (each 6 oz/170 g) water-packed tuna, drained	2
8	large leaves Bibb lettuce	8

1. In a large bowl, combine garlic, onion, ginger, chili sauce, soy sauce, oil and honey (if using). Add tuna, flaking it and tossing to coat it with sauce.

2. Divide tuna mixture evenly among prepared foil sheets. Fold foil into flat packets and seal edges tightly. Place packets on a baking sheet.

3. Bake in preheated oven for 8 to 10 minutes, turning packets over once, until heated through. Remove from oven and open packets with caution, allowing steam to escape.

4. Spoon tuna mixture into lettuce leaves, dividing evenly. Wrap lettuce leaves around tuna mixture.

Crab- and Shrimp-Stuffed Sole

Makes 4 servings

This dish is the ultimate gourmet entrée. A delicately seasoned crab, shrimp and cream cheese filling is rolled into light and flaky sole fillets, for a scrumptious meal that will have your dinner guests raving.

Tip

One medium lemon (about 6 oz/175 g) yields about 2 tbsp (30 mL) juice and 1 tbsp (15 mL) zest. If you zest the whole lemon, you can save the remaining zest for later by adding 1 tsp (5 mL) to each of two cups in a miniature ice cube tray. Cover with water and freeze until ready to use.

- Preheat oven to 350°F (180°C)
- 4 sheets heavy-duty foil, sprayed with nonstick cooking spray
- 4 toothpicks

1	can (6 oz/170 g) crabmeat, drained and flaked	1
½ cup	chopped cooked shrimp	125 mL
¼ cup	fresh bread crumbs	60 mL
2 tsp	minced fresh chives	10 mL
1 tsp	minced fresh parsley	5 mL
1 tsp	grated lemon zest	5 mL
1	clove garlic, minced	1
¼ cup	butter, melted, divided	60 mL
2 tbsp	whipped cream cheese spread	30 mL
1½ cups	quartered cherry tomatoes	375 mL
½ tsp	kosher salt	2 mL
½ tsp	freshly ground black pepper	2 mL
2 tbsp	dry white wine	30 mL
2 tbsp	freshly squeezed lemon juice	30 mL
4	skinless sole fillets (each about 6 oz/175 g)	4

1. In a small bowl, combine crab, shrimp, bread crumbs, chives, parsley, lemon zest, garlic, 2 tbsp (30 mL) butter and cream cheese.

2. In a large bowl, combine tomatoes, salt, pepper, wine, lemon juice and the remaining butter.

3. Place a sole fillet on each prepared foil sheet. Spoon crab mixture onto each fillet, covering the fish to within ½ inch (1 cm) of the edges. Roll up fillets around filling and secure with toothpicks (being careful not to poke foil). Top with tomato mixture, dividing evenly. Remove toothpicks and fold foil into flat packets, sealing edges tightly. Place packets on a baking sheet.

4. Bake in preheated oven for 12 to 15 minutes or until fish is opaque and flakes easily when tested with a fork.

Zesty Roasted Soft-Shell Crab

One of North America's favorite delicacies, these soft-shell crabs are accompanied by a zesty aïoli that is an especially delectable treat.

Tips

Soft-shell crab season in the U.S. runs from April through October. For the best crabs, buy them during this season. Soft-shell crabs have molted their old, harder shell. They are soft for about 2 to 3 hours. The ideal crabs are harvested during this time.

Choose crabs that are not wrapped in cellophane, as those have most likely been frozen. Look for crabs with a soft shell, not a paper shell. They should have all of their legs and claws.

To clean soft-shell crabs, hold each crab in one hand and use kitchen shears to cut about ½ inch (1 cm) off the front of the crab, behind the eyes and mouth. Squeeze out the exposed sac. Lift the pointed ends of the crab's shell and remove and discard gills. Turn the crab over and cut off the small flap underneath. Rinse crab well and pat dry.

- Preheat oven to 500°F (260°C)
- 4 double sheets heavy-duty foil, top sheets sprayed with nonstick cooking spray

1	clove garlic, minced	1
1 tbsp	butter, melted	15 mL
1 tbsp	virgin olive oil	15 mL
4	large soft-shell crabs, cleaned (see tips, at left)	4
2 tbsp	mayonnaise	30 mL
1 tsp	freshly squeezed lemon juice	5 mL
Pinch	chili powder	Pinch
	Kosher salt	
1	lemon, cut into wedges	1

1. In a small bowl, combine garlic, butter and oil.

2. Place a crab on each prepared foil sheet. Brush garlic mixture over crabs. Fold foil into flat packets and seal edges tightly. Place packets on a baking sheet.

3. Roast in preheated oven for 8 to 10 minutes or until crackling and nicely browned.

4. Meanwhile, in a small bowl, combine mayonnaise, lemon juice and chili powder. Season to taste with salt.

5. Serve crabs with sauce and lemon wedges on the side.

Coconut Lime Shrimp with Plantains and Mango Salsa

|||||||||||||||||||||||||||||||||||||||||||||||||||||||||||||||||||||||||||||||||||||||||||||||||||||||||||||||||||||||||||||||||||||||||||||||||||||||||||||||||||

Transport yourself to a Caribbean island with the fresh taste of shrimp, delicately flavored with coconut and lime and paired with a delectable mango salsa.

Tips

Be sure to grate the zest from the lime before squeezing the juice for the salsa. The zest will be added to the coconut shrimp.

If you can't find frozen fried sweet plantains and want to make your own, cut 3 well-ripened plantains diagonally into slices about ¼ inch (0.5 cm) thick. Lightly coat plantain slices in brown sugar. In a skillet, heat about ¼ inch (0.5 cm) of vegetable oil over high heat. Add plantain slices and cook, turning once, for 2 minutes or until crispy on both sides. Add to the foil packets as directed in step 3.

- Preheat oven to 350°F (180°C)
- 4 sheets heavy-duty foil, sprayed with nonstick cooking spray

Mango Salsa

2	small plum (Roma) tomatoes, diced	2
1	large ripe but firm mango, diced	1
1	jalapeño pepper, seeded and finely chopped	1
½	small jicama, peeled and finely chopped (about ½ cup/125 mL)	½
2 tbsp	freshly squeezed lime juice (see tip, at left)	30 mL
1 tsp	extra virgin olive oil	5 mL
	Kosher salt	
¼ cup	chopped fresh cilantro	60 mL

Coconut Lime Shrimp

2 lbs	large shrimp, peeled and deveined	1 kg
⅔ cup	coconut milk	150 mL
	Grated zest of 1 lime	
1	package (10 oz/300 g) frozen fried sweet plantains, thawed (see tip, at left)	1

1. *Salsa:* In a medium bowl, combine tomatoes, mango, jalapeño, jicama, lime juice and oil. Season to taste with salt. Let stand for 15 to 20 minutes.

2. *Shrimp:* Meanwhile, in a large bowl, toss shrimp with coconut milk and lime zest.

3. Divide plantains among prepared foil sheets. Top with shrimp, dividing evenly. Fold foil into flat packets and seal edges tightly. Place packets on a baking sheet.

4. Bake in preheated oven for 10 minutes or until shrimp are pink, firm and opaque.

5. Serve shrimp and plantains sprinkled with cilantro, with mango salsa on the side.

Shrimp Creole with Crispy Cornbread Dippers

Makes 4 servings

This shrimp Creole dish, a Louisiana favorite, is deeply flavored with a tomato-based hot sauce and the holy trinity of onions, celery and peppers. It is served with crispy cornbread for dipping in the rich sauce.

- Preheat oven to 400°F (200°C)
- 9-inch (23 cm) square metal baking pan, greased
- 4 double sheets heavy-duty foil, top sheets sprayed with nonstick cooking spray

1	package (8½ oz/250 g) cornbread mix	1
4	cloves garlic, minced	4
3	onions, chopped	3
2	stalks celery, chopped	2
1	green bell pepper, chopped	1
Pinch	cayenne pepper	Pinch
2	bay leaves	2
1	can (14 oz/398 mL) tomato sauce	1
1 cup	seafood stock or ready-to-use vegetable broth	250 mL
¼ cup	butter, melted	60 mL
Dash	Worcestershire sauce	Dash
Dash	hot pepper sauce	Dash
	Kosher salt and freshly ground black pepper	
2 cups	cooked long-grain white rice	500 mL
2 lbs	extra-large shrimp (26 to 30 count), peeled and deveined	1 kg
¼ cup	sliced green onions	60 mL

1. Prepare cornbread mix according to package directions. Pour batter into prepared baking pan. Bake in preheated oven for 15 minutes or until top is golden. Remove from oven, leaving oven on, and let cool for 10 minutes or until easy to touch.

2. Cut cornbread into 3- by 1-inch (7.5 by 2.5 cm) slices. Arrange slices on a baking sheet and bake for 8 to 10 minutes, turning once, until crispy and golden. Transfer cornbread slices to a plate and set aside.

3. In a large bowl, combine garlic, onions, celery, green pepper, cayenne, bay leaves, tomato sauce, seafood stock, butter, Worcestershire sauce and hot pepper sauce. Season to taste with salt and black pepper.

Tip

The cornbread dippers can be prepared ahead of time. Store at room temperature, lightly wrapped in parchment or waxed paper. Any leftover dippers can also be stored this way, for up to 2 days.

4. Fold each prepared foil sheet into a bowl shape. Add ½ cup (125 mL) rice to the bottom of each "bowl." Top with Creole mixture, dividing evenly. Fold foil into tent-style packets and seal edges tightly. Place packets on baking sheet.

5. Bake for 20 minutes, rotating packets a half-turn halfway through, until rice is heated through.

6. Reduce oven temperature to 350°F (180°C). Carefully, to avoid tearing foil, open packets, allowing steam to escape. Divide shrimp evenly among packets, pressing shrimp down into sauce. Reseal packets and bake for 3 to 5 minutes or until shrimp are pink, firm and opaque.

7. Serve garnished with green onions, with cornbread dippers on the side.

Basil and Garlic Chicken with Braised Pears and Fennel

||||||||||||||||||||||||||||||||||||||||||||||||||||||||||||||||||||||||||||||||||||||||||||||||||||||||||||||||||||||||

Makes 4 servings

These basil- and garlic-marinated breasts are moist and mouthwatering. When paired with glazed pears and fennel, they hit even higher notes of flavor.

Tip

For best results, use pears that are neither over- nor under-ripe.

- Preheat oven to 375°F (190°C)
- 8 sheets heavy-duty foil, sprayed with nonstick cooking spray

4	cloves garlic, minced	4
¼ cup	chopped fresh basil	60 mL
¼ cup	virgin olive oil, divided	60 mL
4	boneless skinless chicken breasts (each about 4 oz/125 g)	4
	Kosher salt and freshly ground black pepper	
1 cup	balsamic vinegar	250 mL
¼ cup	light (fancy) molasses	60 mL
4	firm ripe pears, cut in half, stems and pith removed	4
1	small bulb fennel, cut into 8 wedges	1

1. In a small bowl, combine garlic, basil and 2 tbsp (30 mL) oil. Brush over both sides of chicken. Season with salt and pepper.

2. Place a chicken breast in center of each of 4 prepared foil sheets. Fold foil into tent-style packets and seal edges tightly. Place packets, fold side up, on a baking sheet. Refrigerate while preparing the glaze (or for up to 6 hours).

3. In a small saucepan, bring vinegar to a boil over medium-high heat. Reduce heat and simmer for 15 to 20 minutes or until reduced by half. Remove from heat and stir in molasses and 1 tbsp (15 mL) pepper.

4. Brush pears and fennel with the remaining oil. Place 2 pear halves and 2 fennel wedges, cut side up, on each of the remaining prepared foil sheets. Brush the tops of the pears and fennel with some of the glaze. Fold foil into flat packets and seal edges tightly. Set aside. Keep the remaining glaze warm.

Tip

For variety, substitute fully ripe peaches for the pears.

5. Use baking sheet to transfer chicken packets to the preheated oven, sliding packets off the sheet and onto the oven rack. Bake for 12 minutes. Turn chicken packets over and add pear packets, fold side down, to the oven. Bake for 3 minutes. Turn pear packets over and bake for 3 minutes. Remove pear packets from oven and let stand until chicken is done. Continue baking chicken for 2 to 4 minutes or until chicken is no longer pink inside.

6. Brush pears and fennel with more glaze and serve alongside chicken. Serve any remaining glaze on the side for drizzling over the chicken or the pears and fennel.

Santa Fe Chicken and Rice

This chicken dish is flavorful, colorful and oh so satisfying. What more could you ask for?

Tip
You can substitute 2 cans (each 8 oz/227 mL) corn kernels, drained, for the frozen corn.

- Preheat oven to 425°F (220°C)
- 4 double sheets heavy-duty foil, top sheets sprayed with nonstick cooking spray

1	can (14 to 19 oz/398 to 540 mL) black beans, drained and rinsed	1
2 cups	frozen corn kernels	500 mL
1	can (10 oz/284 mL) diced tomatoes, drained	1
1	can (4½ oz/127 mL) diced green chiles	1
½ tsp	ground cumin	2 mL
4	boneless skinless chicken breasts (each about 4 oz/125 g)	4
2 cups	cooked white rice	500 mL
½ cup	shredded Mexican cheese blend	125 mL

1. In a medium bowl, combine beans, corn, tomatoes, chiles and cumin.

2. Place a chicken breast on each prepared foil sheet. Spoon bean mixture over top, dividing evenly. Arrange rice around chicken. Fold foil into tent-style packets and seal edges tightly. Place packets on a baking sheet.

3. Bake in preheated oven for 15 to 20 minutes or until chicken is no longer pink inside.

4. Remove from oven and open packets with caution, allowing steam to escape. Sprinkle with cheese and loosely close packets, without touching cheese. Let stand for 2 minutes or until cheese is melted.

Paprika Chicken with Baby Vegetables

In this delectable comfort-food dish, chicken and sweet, delicate vegetables are covered in a creamy gravy seasoned with paprika and thyme.

Tip

In place of the chicken gravy and flour, you could use a 12-oz (340 mL) can of condensed cream of mushroom or cream of celery soup.

- Preheat oven to 400°F (200°C)
- 4 double sheets heavy-duty foil, top sheets sprayed with nonstick cooking spray

1 cup	chicken gravy	250 mL
2 tbsp	all-purpose flour	30 mL
4	boneless skinless chicken breasts (each about 4 oz/125 g)	4
5	small red-skinned potatoes, quartered	5
1½ cups	baby carrots, cut in half lengthwise	375 mL
1 cup	frozen French-cut green beans	250 mL
1 tsp	paprika	5 mL
1 tsp	dried thyme	5 mL
2 tbsp	finely chopped fresh parsley	30 mL

1. In a small bowl, combine gravy and flour until well blended.

2. Place a chicken breast on each prepared foil sheet. Top with potatoes, carrots and green beans, dividing evenly. Fold edges of foil up into a bowl shape around the chicken. Drizzle gravy mixture over vegetables. Sprinkle with paprika and thyme. Fold foil into tent-style packets and seal edges tightly. Place packets on a baking sheet.

3. Bake in preheated oven for 25 to 30 minutes, rotating packets a half-turn halfway through, until chicken is no longer pink inside and vegetables are tender. Serve sprinkled with parsley.

Curry Coconut Chicken with Zucchini and Carrots

You are sure to enjoy the Indian- and Turkish-inspired flavors of this delectable chicken and vegetable dish.

Tip

If your chicken breasts vary a lot in thickness, place them between 2 sheets of plastic wrap and, using a meat mallet or rolling pin, pound them to an even thickness.

- Preheat oven to 350°F (180°C)
- Blender
- 4 sheets heavy-duty foil, sprayed with nonstick cooking spray

2	green onions, sliced	2
1	large banana	1
1 tbsp	grated gingerroot	15 mL
1 tsp	curry powder	5 mL
½ tsp	ground turmeric	2 mL
¼ tsp	ground cinnamon	1 mL
⅛ tsp	cayenne pepper	0.5 mL
½ cup	coconut milk	125 mL
2	carrots, sliced	2
1	red bell pepper, sliced	1
1	large zucchini, sliced	1
4	boneless skinless chicken breasts (each about 4 oz/125 g)	4
	Kosher salt and freshly ground black pepper	
	Chopped fresh cilantro	

1. In blender, combine green onions, banana, ginger, curry powder, turmeric, cinnamon, cayenne and coconut milk; process until smooth.

2. Divide carrots, red pepper and zucchini evenly among prepared foil sheets. Top with chicken and season with salt and pepper. Fold edges of foil up into a bowl shape around the vegetables and chicken. Pour coconut milk mixture over chicken, dividing evenly. Fold foil into tent-style packets and seal edges tightly. Place packets on a baking sheet.

3. Bake in preheated oven for 22 to 25 minutes or until chicken is no longer pink inside.

4. Transfer chicken and vegetables to plates and spoon sauce over top. Garnish with cilantro.

Garam Masala Chicken and Vegetables

Makes 4 servings

This Indian-inspired dish is impeccably seasoned with a perfect balance of flavors.

Tip

Remove the center stems from the cilantro for a milder and less intense flavor.

- Preheat oven to 350°F (180°C)
- 4 sheets heavy-duty foil, sprayed with nonstick cooking spray

4	cloves garlic, minced	4
2 tbsp	garam masala, divided	30 mL
1 tsp	kosher salt	5 mL
½ tsp	freshly ground black pepper	2 mL
¼ cup	virgin olive oil	60 mL
4	boneless skinless chicken breasts (each about 4 oz/125 g)	4
4	yellow summer squash, cut into ¼-inch (0.5 cm) rounds	4
1	Vidalia onion, thinly sliced	1
½ cup	plain Greek yogurt	125 mL
	Fresh cilantro leaves	

1. In a small bowl, combine garlic, 1½ tbsp (22 mL) garam masala, salt, pepper and oil.

2. Place a chicken breast on each prepared foil sheet. Sprinkle both sides of breasts with the remaining garam masala. Top with squash and onion, dividing evenly. Drizzle evenly with garlic mixture. Fold foil into tent-style packets and seal edges tightly. Place packets on a baking sheet.

3. Bake in preheated oven for 22 to 25 minutes or until chicken is no longer pink inside. Serve dolloped with yogurt and sprinkled with cilantro.

Chicken with Peanut Sauce and Sweet Potatoes

You will love the rich and creamy flavors of peanut butter, sweet coconut, citrus and a bit of spice that accompany the chicken, sweet potatoes and green beans in this Asian-inspired dish.

Tip

If you prefer to omit the sweet potatoes, use an additional 6 oz (175 g) green beans.

- Preheat oven to 450°F (230°C)
- 4 double sheets heavy-duty foil, top sheets sprayed with nonstick cooking spray

1	clove garlic, minced	1
3 tbsp	chopped fresh cilantro, divided	45 mL
1 tbsp	minced gingerroot	15 mL
1 tsp	hot pepper flakes	5 mL
¼ cup	unsalted creamy peanut butter	60 mL
¼ cup	coconut milk	60 mL
2 tbsp	unseasoned rice vinegar	30 mL
1 tbsp	liquid honey	15 mL
1 tbsp	freshly squeezed lime juice	15 mL
1 tsp	tamari	5 mL
12 oz	green beans, trimmed	375 g
2	sweet potatoes, peeled and cut into ½-inch (1 cm) cubes	2
1	red onion, thinly sliced	1
1 lb	boneless skinless chicken breasts, cut into 1-inch (2.5 cm) pieces	500 g

1. In a medium bowl, whisk together garlic, 2 tbsp (30 mL) cilantro, ginger, hot pepper flakes, peanut butter, coconut milk, vinegar, honey, lime juice and tamari.

2. Divide green beans, sweet potatoes and onion evenly among prepared foil sheets. Top with chicken, dividing evenly. Drizzle evenly with peanut sauce. Fold foil into tent-style packets and seal edges tightly. Place packets on a baking sheet.

3. Bake in preheated oven for 10 to 15 minutes or until chicken is no longer pink inside and vegetables are tender. Serve garnished with the remaining cilantro.

Variation

Substitute an equal weight of pork tenderloin cubes for the chicken.

Sweet-and-Sour Chicken and Mushrooms

Baking this traditional sweet-and-sour chicken dish in foil results in super-moist and tender chicken without the hassle of cleaning up a wok.

Tip

If you prefer, you can use 1 cup (250 mL) cubed fresh pineapple in place of canned.

- Preheat oven to 350°F (180°C)
- 4 sheets heavy-duty foil, sprayed with nonstick cooking spray

1 lb	boneless skinless chicken breasts, cut into 1-inch (2.5 cm) pieces	500 g
½ cup	sweet-and-sour sauce	125 mL
1	can (8 oz/227 mL) pineapple chunks, drained	1
1	green bell pepper, cut into strips	1
8 oz	mushrooms, sliced	250 g
1 cup	crispy chow mein noodles	250 mL

1. Divide chicken evenly among prepared foil sheets. Drizzle each with 1 tbsp (15 mL) sauce. Top with pineapple, green pepper and mushrooms, dividing evenly. Drizzle evenly with the remaining sauce. Fold foil into tent-style packets and seal edges tightly. Place packets on a baking sheet.

2. Bake in preheated oven for 15 to 20 minutes, rotating packets a quarter-turn halfway through, until chicken is no longer pink inside. Serve topped with chow mein noodles.

Variation

Substitute 1 cup (250 mL) small broccoli florets for the green pepper.

Cream of Mushroom Chicken and Wild Rice with Peppers

||||||||||||||||||||||||||||||||||||||||||||||||||||||||||||||||||||||||||||||||||||||||||||||||||||||||||||||||||||||

Makes 6 servings

If it's a creamy and cheesy comfort food dish you're looking for, you will surely want to make this one: a combination of chicken, wild rice and a cornucopia of peppers, onions and celery, all covered with a creamy mushroom sauce.

Tips

A typical rotisserie chicken weighs about 2½ lbs (1.25 kg) and will yield about 4 cups (1 L) shredded chicken.

Pick up your rotisserie chicken at the end of your grocery shopping trip. Use it within 2 hours or refrigerate and use within 3 days.

- Preheat oven to 350°F (180°C)
- 6 sheets heavy-duty foil, sprayed with nonstick cooking spray

⅓ cup	butter	75 mL
1 cup	chopped onions	250 mL
1	green bell pepper, chopped	1
1	red bell pepper, chopped	1
1	stalk celery, chopped	1
1	rotisserie chicken, deboned, skin removed and meat shredded	1
1	package (6 oz/175 g) wild rice mix, cooked	1
1 cup	shredded Cheddar cheese	250 mL
1 cup	shredded Swiss cheese	250 mL
1	can (10 oz/284 mL) condensed cream of mushroom soup	1
	Kosher salt and freshly ground black pepper	

1. In a medium skillet, melt butter over medium heat. Add onions, green pepper, red pepper and celery; cook, stirring, for 7 to 9 minutes or until softened.

2. In a large bowl, combine onion mixture, chicken, rice, Cheddar, Swiss cheese and mushroom soup. Season to taste with salt and pepper.

3. Fold each prepared foil sheet into a bowl shape. Divide chicken mixture evenly among "bowls." Fold foil into tent-style packets and seal edges tightly. Place packets on a baking sheet.

4. Bake in preheated oven for 20 minutes or until heated through.

Rotisserie Chicken, Bean and Corn Tacos

Makes 6 servings

So simple to prepare, these savory tacos are made with ready-to-go ingredients, so all you need to do is assemble, bake and enjoy.

Tips

A typical rotisserie chicken weighs about 2½ lbs (1.25 kg) and will yield about 4 cups (1 L) shredded chicken.

Pick up your rotisserie chicken at the end of your grocery shopping trip. Use it within 2 hours or refrigerate and use within 3 days.

The foil packets can be prepared through step 2 and refrigerated for up to 2 days or frozen for up to 1 month. If frozen, thaw in the refrigerator overnight before baking.

- Preheat oven to 350°F (180°C)
- 6 double sheets heavy-duty foil, top sheets sprayed with nonstick cooking spray

1	rotisserie chicken, deboned, skin removed and meat shredded	1
1	can (14 to 19 oz/398 to 540 mL) black beans, drained and rinsed	1
1	can (15 oz/425 mL) corn kernels with diced peppers	1
½ tsp	ground cumin	2 mL
Pinch	kosher salt	Pinch
6	6-inch (15 cm) corn tortillas	6
½ cup	shredded Monterey Jack cheese	125 mL

1. In a large bowl, combine chicken, beans, corn, cumin and salt.

2. Place a tortilla on each prepared foil sheet. Divide chicken mixture evenly among tortillas, making a rectangular shape in the center of the tortilla. Roll up tortillas. Fold foil into flat packets and seal edges tightly. Place packets on a baking sheet.

3. Bake in preheated oven for 35 to 40 minutes, turning packets over occasionally, until heated through. Remove from oven and open packets with caution, allowing steam to escape. Sprinkle with cheese and loosely close packets, without touching cheese. Let stand for 2 minutes or until cheese is slightly melted.

Southern Hot Brown Single-Serve Casseroles

Makes 4 servings

Talk about comfort food — this Kentucky favorite is bursting with flavor. Turkey, tomatoes and bacon are smothered in a creamy cheese sauce that will melt in your mouth.

Tips

In place of the Texas toast, you can use any dense, firm bread, such as sourdough.

To mix things up, substitute sliced deli ham for half of the turkey.

- Preheat oven to 350°F (180°C)
- 4 double sheets heavy-duty foil, top sheets sprayed with nonstick cooking spray

2 tbsp	butter	30 mL
2 tbsp	all-purpose flour	30 mL
2 cups	milk	500 mL
½ cup	shredded sharp (old) white Cheddar cheese, divided	125 mL
	Kosher salt and freshly ground black pepper	
4	slices Texas toast, crusts removed	4
12 oz	sliced deli roast turkey breast	375 g
2	plum (Roma) tomatoes, sliced and ends discarded	2
8	slices bacon	8
	Paprika	
	Chopped fresh parsley	

1. In a medium saucepan, melt butter over medium heat. Whisk in flour and cook, whisking constantly, for 2 minutes. Whisk in milk and cook, whisking constantly, for 6 to 8 minutes or until sauce is smooth and thickened. Add ¼ cup (60 mL) cheese and stir until melted. Remove from heat and season to taste with salt and pepper.

2. Place a slice of bread on each prepared foil sheet. Top with turkey and tomatoes, dividing evenly. Fold edges of foil up into a bowl shape. Spoon sauce over top, dividing evenly. Sprinkle each with 1½ tsp (7 mL) cheese. Fold foil into tent-style packets and seal edges tightly. Place packets on a baking sheet.

3. Bake in preheated oven for 30 to 35 minutes or until turkey is hot and cheese sauce is bubbling.

4. Meanwhile, in a large skillet, over medium-high heat, cook bacon, turning occasionally, for 7 to 9 minutes or until crispy.

5. Open packets with caution, allowing steam to escape, and crisscross 2 slices of bacon on top of each hot brown. Sprinkle with the remaining cheese, paprika and parsley.

Hoisin-Glazed Country-Style Ribs with Green Beans and Crispy Leeks

Makes 6 servings

A unique and surprising combination of hoisin sauce and blackberry preserves gives a whole new dimension of flavor to country-style pork ribs.

Tips

Raspberry or blueberry preserves would also be delicious in place of the blackberry preserves.

If you can only find bone-in country-style ribs, you'll need 2 lbs (1 kg). When placing them on the foil, take care that the bones do not pierce the foil.

- Preheat oven to 350°F (180°C)
- 6 sheets heavy-duty foil, sprayed with nonstick cooking spray

2	cloves garlic, minced	2
1 tsp	minced gingerroot	5 mL
½ tsp	hot pepper flakes	2 mL
½ tsp	kosher salt	2 mL
¼ tsp	freshly ground black pepper	1 mL
½ cup	blackberry preserves	125 mL
¼ cup	hoisin sauce	60 mL
2 tbsp	red wine vinegar	30 mL
1½ lbs	boneless country-style pork ribs, cut into 6 equal pieces	750 g
1 lb	green beans, trimmed	500 g
1 tbsp	virgin olive oil, divided	15 mL
1	small leek (white and light green parts only), thinly sliced into rings	1

1. In a medium bowl, combine garlic, ginger, hot pepper flakes, salt, pepper, preserves, hoisin sauce and vinegar.

2. Place a piece of pork on each prepared foil sheet. Coat all sides of pork with sauce.

3. In a bowl, toss green beans with half the oil. Arrange around pork, dividing evenly. Fold foil into tent-style packets and seal edges tightly. Place packets on a baking sheet.

4. Bake in preheated oven for 25 to 35 minutes or until pork is fork-tender. Remove packets from oven and let rest, without opening, for 10 minutes.

5. Meanwhile, in a medium skillet, heat the remaining oil over medium-high heat. Add leek and cook, stirring and separating rings, until slightly crispy. Using a slotted spoon, transfer leek rings to a plate lined with paper towels.

6. Transfer pork to plates, drizzle with sauce from foil and garnish with crispy leeks. Serve green beans on the side.

Juicy Herb-Roasted Pork Loin with Ginger Carrots and Parsnips

Makes 6 servings

This sweet and savory marinated pork loin comes out juicy and tender every time because we seal in the juices. Served with ginger carrots and parsnips, you have a gratifying meal in a packet.

- Triple sheet heavy-duty foil, top sheet sprayed with nonstick cooking spray

6	cloves garlic, minced	6
1½ tbsp	minced fresh rosemary	22 mL
1 tbsp	chopped fresh thyme	15 mL
1 tbsp	grated lemon zest	15 mL
	Juice of 4 lemons (about ½ cup/ 125 mL)	
⅓ cup	virgin olive oil, divided	75 mL
2 tbsp	soy sauce	30 mL
2 tbsp	liquid honey	30 mL
1	large (1¼- to 1½-lb/625 to 750 mL) pork tenderloin, trimmed	1
	Kosher salt and freshly ground black pepper	
4	carrots, thinly sliced	4
4	parsnips, thinly sliced	4
2 tsp	grated gingerroot	10 mL

1. In a large sealable plastic bag, combine garlic, rosemary, thyme, lemon zest, lemon juice, 3 tbsp (45 mL) oil, soy sauce and honey. Seal and shake bag to blend. Add pork, seal and turn bag to coat pork with marinade. Refrigerate for at least 2 hours or up to 6 hours.

2. Preheat oven to 400°F (200°C).

3. Place prepared foil sheet on a baking sheet. Remove pork from marinade, discarding marinade, and place in center of foil. Season with salt and pepper.

4. In a medium bowl, toss together carrots, parsnips, ginger and the remaining oil. Arrange vegetables around pork. Fold foil into a tent-style packet and seal edges tightly.

Tip

If you zest all 4 lemons, you will have about 3 tbsp (45 mL) zest remaining. Save it for later use by adding 1 tsp (5 mL) to each cup in a miniature ice cube tray. Cover with water and freeze until ready to use.

5. Use baking sheet to transfer the packet to the oven, sliding it off the sheet and onto the oven rack. Roast for 30 minutes. Open top of packet and roast for 10 to 15 minutes or until an instant-read thermometer inserted in the thickest part of the tenderloin registers 145°F (63°C) for medium-rare (or cook to desired doneness). Slide packet back onto the baking sheet to remove from oven. Reseal packet and let rest for 5 minutes.

6. Transfer pork to a cutting board and slice across the grain. Serve with carrots and parsnips.

Pork Tenderloin in Garlic Mushroom Cream Sauce

	Makes 4 servings	

Make your taste buds happy with these tender fillets topped with a creamy mushroom Alfredo sauce.

Tips

You can use ready-to-use chicken broth in place of the wine, if you prefer. You may wish to omit the salt from the recipe unless your broth is low in sodium.

Serve this dish with Roasted Artichokes with Garlic Crumbs (page 190) for a delicious complete meal.

- Preheat oven to 325°F (160°C)
- Triple sheet heavy-duty foil, top sheet sprayed with nonstick cooking spray

8 oz	mushrooms, sliced	250 g
1	clove garlic, minced	1
1⅔ cups	Alfredo sauce	400 mL
½ cup	dry white wine	125 mL
2 tbsp	butter, melted	30 mL
1 lb	pork tenderloin, trimmed	500 g
	Kosher salt and freshly ground black pepper	

1. In a medium bowl, combine mushrooms, garlic, Alfredo sauce, wine and butter.

2. Place prepared foil sheet on a baking sheet. Place pork in center of foil. Fold edges of foil up into a bowl shape around the pork. Drizzle mushroom sauce over pork. Season with salt and pepper. Fold foil into a flat packet and seal edges tightly.

3. Use baking sheet to transfer the packet to the preheated oven, sliding it off the sheet and onto the oven rack. Roast for 45 to 60 minutes, turning packet over occasionally, until an instant-read thermometer inserted in the thickest part of the tenderloin registers 145°F (63°C) for medium-rare (or cook to desired doneness). Slide packet back onto the baking sheet to remove from oven. Let rest, without opening, for 10 minutes.

4. Transfer pork to a cutting board and slice across the grain. Serve drizzled with mushroom sauce.

Five-Spice Pork with Broccoli and Water Chestnuts

If you like spice in your stir-fries, you will love the infusion of flavors in this pork and broccoli dish. The water chestnuts add a slight refreshing crunch to the savory pork.

- Preheat oven to 400°F (200°C)
- 4 double sheets heavy-duty foil, top sheets sprayed with nonstick cooking spray

1 lb	pork tenderloin, trimmed and cut into 1-inch (2.5 cm) chunks	500 g
3	cloves garlic, minced	3
1	package (16 oz/500 g) frozen broccoli florets	1
1	can (6 oz/170 mL) sliced water chestnuts, drained	1
1 tbsp	Chinese five-spice powder	15 mL
¼ cup	virgin olive oil, divided	60 mL
1 tbsp	soy sauce	15 mL
	Kosher salt	

1. In a large bowl, toss together pork, garlic, broccoli, water chestnuts, five-spice powder, oil and soy sauce. Season with salt.

2. Divide pork mixture evenly among prepared foil sheets. Fold foil into tent-style packets and seal edges tightly. Place packets on a baking sheet.

3. Bake in preheated oven for 15 to 18 minutes, turning packets over and rotating them occasionally, until just a hint of pink remains in pork and broccoli is done to your liking. Serve immediately.

Variation

Substitute boneless skinless chicken breasts chunks for the pork and bake the packets for 15 to 18 minutes or until chicken is no longer pink inside.

Spicy Szechuan Pork Bundles

||||||||||||||||||||||||||||||||||||||||||||||||||||||||||||||||||||||||||||||||||||||||||||||||||||||||||||||||||||||||||||||||||||||||||||||||||||||

A spicy chili garlic
sauce and fresh ginger
imbue mini pork balls,
peppers and noodles
with an explosion of
flavors and textures
you will enjoy.

Tip

The soba noodles can be
replaced with another one of
your favorite Asian noodles,
such as udon or somen.

- Preheat oven to 375°F (190°C)
- 4 double sheets heavy-duty foil, top sheets sprayed with nonstick cooking spray

1	small red bell pepper, cut into strips	1
1 tsp	grated gingerroot	5 mL
¼ cup	ready-to-use chicken broth	60 mL
1½ tbsp	soy sauce	22 mL
1 tbsp	chili garlic sauce	15 mL
1 tbsp	creamy peanut butter	15 mL
2 tsp	toasted sesame oil	10 mL
1 lb	ground pork	500 g
6 oz	soba noodles	175 g
4	green onions, cut into diagonal slices	4

1. In a medium bowl, combine red pepper, ginger, broth, soy sauce, chili garlic sauce, peanut butter and oil.

2. Form pork into 1-inch (2.5 cm) diameter balls. Divide balls evenly among prepared foil sheets. Fold edges of foil up into a bowl shape around the pork. Pour sauce over pork, dividing evenly. Fold foil into flat packets and seal edges tightly. Place packets on a baking sheet.

3. Bake in preheated oven for 12 to 15 minutes, turning packets over once, until just a hint of pink remains in pork and peppers are tender.

4. Meanwhile, cook soba noodles according to package directions. Drain, rinse with hot water and drain again.

5. Serve noodles topped with Szechuan pork mixture. Garnish with green onions.

Variation

Substitute 1 cup (250 mL) small broccoli florets for the red pepper.

Dijon Ham and Swiss Cheese Loaf

This pull-apart ham and Swiss sandwich loaf makes a great party sandwich to share when you gather with family and friends.

Tips

For a little more zip, you can use pepper Jack cheese in place of the Swiss cheese.

For added heat, tuck in drained canned jalapeño slices with the ham and cheese.

- Preheat oven to 350°F (180°C)
- Double sheet heavy-duty foil, top sheet sprayed with nonstick cooking spray

3 tbsp	butter, softened	45 mL
1 tbsp	Dijon mustard	15 mL
1 tbsp	mayonnaise	15 mL
1	loaf Italian bread (about 12 inches/30 cm long)	1
6	slices Swiss cheese	6
12 oz	thinly sliced deli ham	375 g

1. In a small bowl, combine butter, mustard and mayonnaise.

2. Cut bread into 12 slices, without cutting through to the bottom of the loaf, then place on prepared foil sheet. Spread both sides of every other slice with butter mixture. In between each of the spread sides, tuck in 1 slice of cheese. Divide ham evenly among the sections with the cheese, tucking it in. Fold foil into a flat packet and seal edges tightly. Place packet on a baking sheet.

3. Bake in preheated oven for 15 to 20 minutes, rotating packet often, until cheese is melted and sandwich loaf is heated through. Pull apart sandwiches to serve.

Polish Sausage and Country-Style Potatoes

This dish was one of my favorite meals prepared by my German-Polish grandmother. My recipe updates the classic version by cooking in foil to save on cleanup.

Tip

Serve with warmed sauerkraut with caraway seeds.

- Preheat oven to 350°F (180°C)
- Double sheet heavy-duty foil, top sheet sprayed with nonstick cooking spray

1 lb	fully cooked kielbasa, cut into 2-inch (5 cm) thick slices	500 g
2	large red-skinned potatoes, cut into 1-inch (2.5 cm) cubes	2
1	onion, chopped	1
1 tbsp	virgin olive oil	15 mL
	Kosher salt and freshly ground black pepper	
1 tbsp	fresh rosemary, coarsely chopped	15 mL

1. Place prepared foil sheet on a baking sheet. Place kielbasa, potatoes and onions on foil. Drizzle with oil and season with salt and pepper. Sprinkle with rosemary. Carefully toss ingredients to coat with oil and seasonings. Fold foil into a flat packet and seal edges tightly.

2. Bake in preheated oven for 20 to 30 minutes or until potatoes are tender and kielbasa is heated through.

Beef Tenderloin with Glazed Carrots and Parsnips

||||||||||||||||||||||||||||||||||||||||||||||||||||||||||||||||||||||||||||||||||||||||||||||||||||||||||||||||||||||||||||||||||||||||||

Makes 8 servings

Always a company favorite, this mouthwatering beef tenderloin gets added flavor with maple syrup–glazed vegetables.

Tip

Serve with a prepared horseradish sauce or coarse honey mustard sauce.

- Preheat oven 350°F (180°C)
- Triple sheet heavy-duty foil, top sheet sprayed with nonstick cooking spray

2 lb	beef tenderloin roast, trimmed	1 kg
3	cloves garlic, minced	3
	Kosher salt and freshly ground black pepper	
4	carrots, cut into ¼-inch (0.5 cm) diagonal slices	4
2	parsnips, cut into ¼-inch (0.5 cm) diagonal slices	2
1	large onion, chopped	1
1	green bell pepper, cut into strips	1
½ cup	ready-to-use chicken broth	125 mL
3 tbsp	pure maple syrup	45 mL
3	sprigs fresh thyme	3

1. Place prepared foil sheet on a baking sheet. Place roast in center of foil. Rub garlic all over roast. Season with salt and pepper. Arrange carrots, parsnips, onion and green peppers around roast. Fold edges of foil up into a bowl shape around the roast and vegetables. Drizzle vegetables with broth and maple syrup. Top with thyme sprigs. Fold foil into a tent-style packet and seal edges tightly.

2. Use baking sheet to transfer the roast to the preheated oven, sliding the packet off the sheet and onto the oven rack. Roast for 25 to 30 minutes, turning packet over halfway through, until an instant-read thermometer inserted in the thickest part of the roast registers 145°F (63°C) for medium-rare (or cook to desired doneness). Slide packet back onto the baking sheet to remove from oven. Let rest, without opening, for 5 minutes.

3. Transfer tenderloin to a cutting board and slice thinly across the grain. Discard thyme sprigs. Serve beef with vegetables.

Italian Beef Tenderloin with Herb and Gorgonzola Butter

||||||||||||||||||||||||||||||||||||||||||||||||||||||||||||||||||||||||||||||||||||||||||||||||||||||||||||||||||||||||||||

Makes 8 servings

Succulent beef tenderloin is roasted to perfection with a zesty combination of Italian-inspired herbs. Top with herb and Gorgonzola butter and serve alongside roasted stuffed tomatoes, and you have a memorable dinner. *Buon appetito.*

• Triple sheet heavy-duty foil, top sheet sprayed with nonstick cooking spray

4 oz	Gorgonzola cheese, rind removed, softened	125 g
¼ cup	unsalted butter, softened	60 mL
1½ tsp	chopped fresh rosemary	7 mL
	Freshly ground black pepper	
2 tsp	granulated beef bouillon	10 mL
2 tsp	paprika	10 mL
1 tsp	cornstarch	5 mL
1 tsp	dried oregano	5 mL
1 tsp	garlic powder	5 mL
2 lb	beef tenderloin roast, trimmed	1 kg
4 tbsp	virgin olive oil, divided	60 mL
2	cloves garlic, finely chopped	2
4 cups	loosely packed fresh parsley leaves, finely chopped	1 L
2 tbsp	capers, drained and chopped	30 mL
1½ tbsp	finely chopped fresh oregano	22 mL
4	firm tomatoes, halved crosswise and seeded	4
3 tbsp	dry bread crumbs	45 mL

1. In a small bowl, combine Gorgonzola, butter and rosemary until smooth. Transfer mixture to a sheet of plastic wrap and roll into a log about 4 inches (10 cm) long. Refrigerate log for at least 1 hour, until firm, or for up to 12 hours.

2. Meanwhile, preheat oven to 375°F (190°C).

3. In a small bowl, combine 1 tbsp (15 mL) pepper, bouillon, paprika, cornstarch, oregano and garlic powder.

4. Place prepared foil sheet on a baking sheet. Place roast in center of foil. Brush 1 tbsp (15 mL) oil all over roast and rub with seasoning mixture.

Tip

An equal amount of chopped drained green olives can be used in place of the capers.

5. In a large bowl, combine garlic, parsley, capers and oregano. Stuff tomatoes with parsley mixture, dividing evenly. Arrange stuffed tomatoes around roast. Season with pepper. Sprinkle bread crumbs over tomatoes and drizzle with the remaining oil. Fold foil into a tent-style packet and seal edges tightly.

6. Use baking sheet to transfer the roast to the preheated oven, sliding the packet off the sheet and onto the oven rack. Roast for 10 to 15 minutes or until an instant-read thermometer inserted in the thickest part of the tenderloin registers 135°F (57°C) for medium-rare (or cook to desired doneness, keeping in mind that the meat continues to cook in step 7).

7. Increase oven temperature to 475°F (240°C). Open packet and roast for 10 minutes, turning roast inside the packet three times, until roast is slightly seared and tomato topping is browned. Slide packet back onto the baking sheet to remove from oven. Transfer roast to a cutting board, cover with foil and let rest for 5 minutes.

8. Slice roast across the grain into $^1/_2$-inch (1 cm) thick slices. Serve topped with slices of herb and Gorgonzola butter, with roasted tomatoes on the side.

Herb-Crusted Sirloin Tip Roast with Rosemary Beets

Makes 6 servings

You will love the infusion of herbs and garlic that wrap this tender roast. Add rosemary beets, and you have a delectable meal that is easy to make and company-worthy.

Tips

You should always brush beet skins to remove any impurities or fibers. If you prefer, you can peel the beets.

Red beets can be used instead of yellow beets, but keep in mind that the juice will bleed its color onto the roast.

- Mini food processor
- Triple sheet of heavy-duty foil, top sheet sprayed with nonstick cooking spray

5	fresh sage leaves	5
3	cloves garlic, roughly chopped	3
2 tbsp	fresh thyme leaves	30 mL
1 tbsp	kosher salt, divided	15 mL
2 tbsp	virgin olive oil, divided	30 mL
3 lb	boneless beef sirloin tip roast	1.5 kg
4	yellow beets, cut into thin wedges	4
1 tbsp	chopped fresh rosemary	15 mL
	Freshly ground black pepper	

1. In food processor, combine sage, garlic, thyme, half the salt and half the oil; process to a paste.

2. Place roast in a large baking dish and rub paste over roast. Cover and refrigerate for at least 3 hours or overnight.

3. Preheat oven to 450°F (230°C).

4. In a medium bowl, toss beets with the remaining oil, the remaining salt and rosemary.

5. Place prepared foil sheet on a baking sheet. Place roast in center of foil. Arrange beets around roast. Season with pepper. Fold foil into a tent-style packet and seal edges tightly.

6. Use baking sheet to transfer the roast to the oven, sliding the packet off the sheet and onto the oven rack. Roast for 15 minutes. Reduce oven temperature to 350°F (180°C) and continue roasting for 45 to 55 minutes or until an instant-read thermometer inserted in the thickest part of the roast registers 140°F (60°C) for medium-rare (or cook to desired doneness). Slide packet back onto the baking sheet to remove from oven. Let rest, without opening, for 15 minutes.

7. Transfer roast to a cutting board and slice across the grain. Serve with beets.

Neapolitan-Style Beef Pizzaiola

Pizzaiola is a traditional Neapolitan-style dish that, roughly translated, means "meat in a pizza style." Here, thin steaks are decadently layered with fresh herbs and tomatoes.

Tip

To make it easier to peel tomatoes, cut a small X in one end of each tomato. Blanch tomatoes in boiling water for 30 to 60 seconds, then plunge them into ice-cold water. The skins will easily peel off.

- Preheat oven 350°F (180°C)
- 4 double sheets heavy-duty foil, top sheets sprayed with nonstick cooking spray

2	potatoes, peeled and cut into thin slices	2
	Kosher salt and freshly ground black pepper	
⅓ cup	virgin olive oil, divided	75 mL
4	slices thin beef flank or skirt steak (each about 4 oz/125 g)	4
1	yellow bell pepper, cut into strips	1
1	green bell pepper, cut into strips	1
4	tomatoes, peeled, seeded and finely chopped	4
4	cloves garlic, chopped	4
1	small onion, finely chopped	1
½ cup	chopped fresh parsley	125 mL
½ cup	chopped fresh oregano	125 mL
¼ cup	drained pickled or brine-packed pepperoncini (optional)	60 mL

1. Arrange potato slices in a rectangular single layer in center of prepared foil sheets, dividing evenly. Season with salt and pepper. Drizzle with half the oil. Add steak on top of the potatoes. Season with salt and pepper. Drizzle with the remaining oil. Top with yellow pepper and green pepper, dividing evenly.

2. In a medium bowl, combine tomatoes, garlic, onion, parsley and oregano. Fold edges of foil up into a bowl shape around the steaks. Add tomato mixture, dividing evenly. Fold foil into tent-style packets and seal edges tightly. Place packets on a baking sheet.

3. Bake in preheated oven for 40 to 50 minutes, rotating packets a quarter-turn twice, until beef is tender and vegetables are softened. If desired, serve garnished with pepperoncini.

Beef Fajita Packets

Makes 8 servings

Sizzling beef fajitas get a makeover with this no-mess recipe. Wrapping the beef mixture in foil and baking it in the oven results in tenderness and an infusion of flavor.

Tips

For warm tortillas, spray 1 large foil sheet with cooking spray. Stack tortillas 2 at a time, separating each pair with a sheet of parchment paper. Fold foil into a flat packet and seal edges tightly. Heat directly on oven rack for 5 to 7 minutes, turning packet over once, until warm.

If desired, you can spread salsa, sour cream and/or guacamole over the tortillas before adding the fajita mixture.

- Preheat oven to 375°F (190°C)
- 8 sheets heavy-duty foil, sprayed with nonstick cooking spray

2 lbs	beef sirloin, cut into 1-inch (2.5 cm) strips	1 kg
4	small tomatoes, cut in half, then sliced	4
2	onions, cut in half, then sliced	2
1	small red bell pepper, sliced	1
1	small green bell pepper, sliced	1
	Dried fajita seasoning mix	
8	burrito size (10-inch/25 cm) flour tortillas (see tip, at left)	8
1 cup	shredded white Cheddar cheese	250 mL

1. In a medium bowl, toss together beef, tomatoes, onions, red pepper and green pepper. Season liberally with fajita seasoning and toss to combine.

2. Divide fajita mixture evenly among prepared foil sheets. Fold foil into flat packets and seal edges tightly. Place packets on a baking sheet.

3. Bake in preheated oven for 35 to 40 minutes, turning packets over occasionally, until beef is tender and vegetables are dark golden brown.

4. Divide fajita mixture evenly among tortillas. Sprinkle with cheese. Tuck in one end of each tortilla and roll to wrap.

184   Oven Recipes: Pork, Beef and Lamb

After-School Hobo Packet

Quick, easy and entirely satisfying as an after-school or after-sports pick-me-up, these packets can be made ahead of time and popped in the oven for 10 minutes.

Tip

Hobo packets can be prepared through step 1 and refrigerated for up to 2 days. Increase the cooking time by 3 minutes.

- Preheat oven to 350°F (180°C)
- Double sheet heavy-duty foil, top sheet sprayed with nonstick cooking spray

1	carrot, sliced	1
1	small potato, peeled and sliced	1
4 oz	beef hamburger patty (store-bought or see recipe, page 186)	125 g
2 tbsp	minced onion (optional)	30 mL
	Kosher salt and freshly ground black pepper	
	Powdered beef gravy mix	

1. Place prepared foil sheet on a baking sheet. Add half the carrot, half the potato and beef patty. Top with the remaining potato and carrot. Sprinkle with onion, if using. Season with salt, pepper and gravy mix. Fold foil into a tent-style packet and seal edges tightly.

2. Bake in preheated oven for 15 minutes or until an instant-read thermometer inserted horizontally into the center of a patty registers 160°F (71°C)and vegetables are tender.

Variation

Substitute 4 oz (125 g) sliced cooked ham, chicken or turkey breast meat for the beef patty.

Make-Ahead Freezer Rainy Day Burgers

These make-ahead burger patties are perfect for those times when you just don't want to grill outside. They are ideal for busy people who want to have a quick and delicious meal ready to go.

Tip

For a flavor twist, use Italian-seasoned dry bread crumbs in place of the plain bread crumbs. Reduce the seasoning salt to 2 tbsp (30 mL).

- 6 sheets heavy-duty foil, sprayed with nonstick cooking spray

1½ lbs	lean ground beef	750 g
¾ cup	dry bread crumbs	175 mL
3 tbsp	seasoning salt	45 mL
⅓ cup	milk	75 mL
1	red onion, sliced and rings separated (optional)	1

Make Ahead

1. In a medium bowl, combine beef, bread crumbs, seasoning salt and milk. Form into six ½-inch (1 cm) thick patties.

2. Place a patty on each prepared foil sheet. Top with onion (if using), dividing evenly. Fold foil into flat packets and seal edges tightly. Refrigerate for up to 2 days or freeze for up to 2 months. (Patties can be thawed in the refrigerator for about 1½ hours before cooking or cooked from frozen.)

When Ready to Cook

3. Preheat oven to 350°F (180°C). Place packets on a baking sheet.

4. Bake thawed patties for 18 to 22 minutes or frozen patties for 25 to 30 minutes, turning packets over once, until an instant-read thermometer inserted horizontally into the center of a patty registers 160°F (71°C).

Pizza Burgers with French-Fried Onions

When you stuff a beef patty with cheese and pizza sauce, you get a kid-friendly pairing of pizza and burgers all wrapped up in one.

Tips

For pepperoni pizza burgers, divide ¼ cup (60 mL) chopped pepperoni evenly on top of the pizza sauce before adding the mozzarella. Omit the salt from the beef patties.

For even more flavor, add 1 tsp (5 mL) sliced ripe olives to the center of each patty after the mozzarella in step 2. Omit the salt from the beef patties.

- Preheat oven to 350°F (180°C)
- 6 sheets heavy-duty foil, sprayed with nonstick cooking spray

2 lbs	lean ground beef	1 kg
½ tsp	kosher salt	2 mL
½ cup	pizza sauce, divided	125 mL
¾ cup	shredded mozzarella cheese	175 mL
6	burger buns, split	6
½ cup	french-fried onions	125 mL

1. Combine beef and salt. Form into 12 thin patties, about 4 inches (10 cm) in diameter.

2. Place 1 patty on each prepared foil sheet. Top center of each with 1 tbsp (15 mL) pizza sauce and sprinkle with mozzarella, dividing evenly. Add another beef patty on top and press edges of beef tightly to seal in filling. Fold foil into flat packets and seal edges tightly. Place packets on a baking sheet.

3. Bake in preheated oven for 20 to 25 minutes, turning packets over once, until an instant-read thermometer inserted horizontally into the center of the meat, avoiding the filling, registers 160°F (71°C).

4. Transfer patties to buns. Top with the remaining pizza sauce and sprinkle with onions.

Tender Roasted Rosemary Garlic Rack of Lamb

Makes 2 servings

Two of my favorite taste-makers, rosemary and garlic, grace this rack of lamb, infusing it with a melodious taste.

Tip

American lamb is typically larger and well marbled. Australian or New Zealand lamb is generally leaner and has a much more intense and often gamey flavor. Either type is incredibly delicious, so use whichever best suits your taste preference and budget.

- Preheat oven to 375°F (190°C)
- 2 sheets heavy-duty foil, sprayed with nonstick cooking spray

1½ lb	rack of lamb, cut into individual chops (see tip, at left)	750 g
2	cloves garlic, cut in half	2
1 tbsp	virgin olive oil	15 mL
	Kosher salt	
1 tbsp	fresh rosemary leaves	15 mL

1. Rub lamb chops all over with the cut side of garlic. Brush both sides of lamb chops with oil. Divide lamb chops evenly among prepared foil sheets. Season with salt and sprinkle with rosemary. Fold foil into flat packets and seal edges tightly. Place packets on a baking sheet.

2. Bake in preheated oven for 20 to 25 minutes, turning packets over once, until an instant-read thermometer inserted in the thickest part of a lamb chop registers 145°F (63°C) for medium-rare (or cook to desired doneness). Remove packets from oven and let rest, without opening, for 5 minutes before serving.

French Onion Baked Lamb Chops

"Simple" and "sensational" are the best words to describe these tender and flavorful lamb chops. So easy to prepare, yet so delectable.

Tip

For added impact, make a small cut in the side of each lamb chop and insert 1 thin slice of fresh garlic before brushing the chops with oil.

- Preheat oven to 375°F (190°C)
- 4 sheets heavy-duty foil, sprayed with nonstick cooking spray

8	lamb chops (each about 2 oz/60 g)	8
	Virgin olive oil	
1	packet (1 oz/28 g) French onion soup mix	1

1. Brush both sides of lamb chops with oil. Place 2 lamb chops in the center of each prepared foil sheet. Sprinkle both sides of lamb chops with soup mix. Fold foil into flat packets and seal edges tightly. Place packets on a baking sheet.

2. Bake in preheated oven for 20 to 25 minutes, turning packets over once, until an instant-read thermometer inserted in the thickest part of a lamb chop registers 145°F (63°C) for medium-rare (or cook to desired doneness). Remove packets from oven and let rest, without opening, for 5 minutes before serving.

Roasted Artichokes with Garlic Crumbs

Sensationally flavored, these roasted artichokes are fun to eat — just pull off individual leaves.

Tip

Serve with lemon wedges, melted butter or aïoli for dipping.

- Preheat oven to 425°F (220°C)
- 2 double sheets heavy-duty foil, top sheets sprayed with nonstick cooking spray

4	cloves garlic, minced	4
⅔ cup	dry bread crumbs	150 mL
½ tsp	kosher salt	2 mL
¼ tsp	freshly ground black pepper	1 mL
¼ tsp	hot pepper flakes	1 mL
	Grated zest and juice of 1 lemon	
2	large artichokes, stem and leaf tips trimmed, chokes scooped out	2
½ cup	virgin olive oil	125 mL

1. In a small bowl, combine garlic, bread crumbs, salt, black pepper, hot pepper flakes and lemon zest.

2. Place an artichoke on each prepared foil sheet. Spread leaves apart. Squeeze lemon juice evenly over top and rub top and sides of each artichoke with lemon. Sprinkle with bread crumb mixture, dividing evenly and opening the leaves to get the mixture down in between them. Drizzle oil over crumbs. Bring the long ends of the foil together, leaving space on top, and fold seams to seal. Fold up the remaining sides and fold seams to seal. Place packets on a baking sheet.

3. Bake in preheated oven for 75 to 90 minutes or until artichokes are tender, leaves pull easily from base and tops are browned and crisp.

Fire-Roasted Broccoli and Cauliflower with Peppers

A vegetable lover's delight, broccoli and cauliflower florets are roasted to perfection and infused with the scrumptious flavors of onions and bell peppers.

Tip

These vegetable packets are a perfect side dish to beef, chicken and pork dishes.

- Preheat oven to 375°F (190°C)
- 4 double sheets heavy-duty foil, top sheets sprayed with nonstick cooking spray

1	red onion, sliced	1
1	red bell pepper, cut into strips	1
1	green bell pepper, cut into strips	1
1	orange bell pepper, cut into strips	1
3 cups	broccoli florets	750 mL
1½ cups	cauliflower florets	375 mL
¼ cup	virgin olive oil	60 mL
1½ tsp	kosher salt	7 mL
1 tsp	freshly ground black pepper	5 mL

1. In a large bowl, toss together onion, red pepper, green pepper, orange pepper, broccoli, cauliflower, oil, salt and pepper.

2. Divide vegetable mixture evenly among prepared foil packets. Fold foil into tent-style packets and seal edges tightly. Places packets on a baking sheet.

3. Bake in preheated oven for 20 to 25 minutes, turning packets over once, until vegetables are tender-crispy and browned.

Cheesy Carrots, Potatoes and Parsnips

You and your family will dig into your vegetables much more readily when they are seasoned to perfection and topped with toasty Parmesan cheese, as in this recipe.

Tip

To change things up, add 1 cup (250 mL) sliced Brussels sprouts to the vegetable mixture.

- Preheat oven to 400°F (200°C)
- 6 double sheets heavy-duty foil, top sheets sprayed with nonstick cooking spray

4	red-skinned potatoes (about 8 oz/ 250 g total), sliced	4
3	carrots, sliced	3
3	parsnips, sliced	3
1	sweet potato, sliced	1
⅓ cup	virgin olive oil	75 mL
1 tbsp	dried oregano	15 mL
1 tbsp	dried rosemary	15 mL
1 tsp	dried thyme	5 mL
1 tsp	dried basil	5 mL
½ tsp	kosher salt	2 mL
¼ tsp	freshly ground black pepper	1 mL
⅓ cup	freshly grated Parmesan cheese	75 mL

1. In a large bowl, toss together potatoes, carrots, parsnips, sweet potato, oil, oregano, rosemary, thyme, basil, salt and pepper.

2. Divide vegetable mixture evenly among prepared foil sheets. Fold foil into tent-style packets and seal edges tightly. Place packets on a baking sheet.

3. Bake in preheated oven for 30 to 35 minutes, turning packets over once, until vegetables are tender. Open packets with caution, allowing steam to escape, and sprinkle evenly with Parmesan. Bake, without resealing, for 5 minutes or until cheese is lightly browned.

Roasted Herb Corn on the Cob

Once you depart from roasting corn the traditional way and try this incredibly flavorful updated version, you will want to make it this way again and again.

Tip

You can substitute 2 tsp (10 mL) dried thyme for the basil, if you prefer.

- Preheat oven to 375°F (190°C)
- 4 double sheets heavy-duty foil, top sheets sprayed with nonstick cooking spray

4	ears sweet corn, shucked	4
⅓ cup	mayonnaise	75 mL
1 tsp	granulated sugar	5 mL
1 tbsp	dried basil	15 mL

1. Brush corn with mayonnaise and sprinkle evenly with sugar and basil. Place a corn cob on each prepared foil sheet. Fold foil loosely around cob and seal edges tightly. Place packets on a baking sheet.

2. Bake in preheated oven for 15 to 20 minutes, turning packets occasionally, until kernels begin to brown and corn is tender.

Variation

If you like a little kick, omit the mayonnaise, sugar and basil. Baste the corn with ¼ cup (60 mL) freshly squeezed lime juice and season to taste with cayenne pepper and kosher salt.

Citrusy Corn Salad

Sweet corn and citrus flavors are teased with cilantro and red onion to bring the flavors of summertime grilling indoors.

Tip

Three limes will yield about ⅓ cup (75 mL) lime juice.

- Preheat oven to 375°F (190°C)
- 4 double sheets heavy-duty foil, top sheets sprayed with nonstick cooking spray

1	bag (16 oz/600 g) frozen corn kernels, thawed	1
1	jar (4 oz/125 g) sliced pimientos, drained	1
1	stalk celery, thinly sliced	1
1 cup	halved grape tomatoes	250 mL
½ cup	finely chopped red onion	125 mL
½ cup	chopped fresh cilantro	125 mL
2 tbsp	granulated sugar	30 mL
1 tbsp	grapeseed oil	15 mL
1 tsp	kosher salt	5 mL
1 tsp	freshly ground black pepper	5 mL
⅓ cup	freshly squeezed lime juice	75 mL
2 tsp	apple cider vinegar	10 mL

1. In a large bowl, combine corn, pimientos, celery, tomatoes, onion, cilantro, sugar and oil.

2. Divide corn mixture evenly among prepared foil sheets. Fold foil into tent-style packets and seal edges tightly. Place packets on a baking sheet.

3. Bake in preheated oven for 8 to 10 minutes or until corn is slightly caramelized. Open packets and let cool completely.

4. In a small bowl, combine salt, pepper, lime juice and vinegar. Drizzle evenly over each portion of corn salad.

Savory Stuffed Onions

Makes 6 servings

If you're a fan of holiday stuffing, you will love these bacon- and mushroom-stuffed onions, packed with flavor.

Tips

Sweet onions such as Vidalia and Walla Walla are perfect for this dish.

You can substitute 2 tsp (10 mL) dried parsley if you don't have fresh parsley on hand.

- Preheat oven to 350°F (180°C)
- 6 double sheets heavy-duty foil, top sheets sprayed with nonstick cooking spray

6	sweet onions (each about 8 oz/ 250 g), peeled	6
4	slices bacon	4
12 oz	mushrooms, sliced	375 g
¼ cup	dry bread crumbs	60 mL
2 tbsp	chopped fresh parsley	30 mL
1 tbsp	butter	15 mL
¼ tsp	kosher salt	1 mL
Pinch	freshly ground black pepper	Pinch
Pinch	ground nutmeg	Pinch
½ cup	ready-to-use beef broth	125 mL

1. In a large pot, bring 1 inch (2.5 cm) of water to a boil over medium-high heat. Using a slotted spoon, place onions, root side down, in pan. Boil for 4 to 6 minutes or until slightly softened. Remove from pan, drain and let cool slightly.

2. Cut off the top quarter of each onion. Remove center of onion, leaving a ½-inch (1 cm) outer shell. Chop the removed onion pieces and set aside.

3. In a medium skillet, over medium heat, cook bacon for 3 to 4 minutes per side, turning once, until slightly crisp. Using tongs, transfer bacon to a plate lined with paper towels to drain, then coarsely chop.

4. Add chopped onion to the bacon drippings in the skillet and cook, stirring, for about 7 minutes or until translucent. Stir in mushrooms, bread crumbs, parsley and butter; cook, stirring, for 3 to 5 minutes or until butter is melted and crumbs are coated. Stir in chopped bacon, salt, pepper and nutmeg. Remove from heat.

5. Place an onion shell on each prepared foil sheet. Stuff bacon mixture into shells, dividing evenly. Fold edges of foil up into a bowl shape around the onions. Pour broth around the bottom of each onion, dividing evenly. Fold foil into tent-style packets and seal edges tightly. Place packets on a baking sheet.

6. Bake in preheated oven for 45 minutes or until onions are tender.

Sweet-and-Savory Butternut Squash Bake

Sweet and succulent butternut squash gets a savory kiss from French onion soup mix, for an elegant side with minimal effort.

Tip

In place of the butternut squash, you could substitute 3 medium acorn squash. Or use 4 small delicata squash and decrease the cooking time to 20 to 25 minutes.

- Preheat oven to 350°F (180°C)
- 6 double sheets heavy-duty foil, top sheets sprayed with nonstick cooking spray

2	small butternut squash, peeled, seeded and cut into 2-inch (5 cm) thick rings	2
2	packets (each 1 oz/28 g) French onion soup mix	2
2 tbsp	packed brown sugar	30 mL
3 tbsp	butter, cut into small pieces	45 mL

1. Divide squash evenly among prepared foil sheets. Sprinkle with onion soup mix and brown sugar. Dot with butter. Fold foil into tent-style packets and seal edges tightly. Place packets on a baking sheet.

2. Bake in preheated oven for 30 to 40 minutes or until squash is tender and dark golden brown.

Bacon Chive Potato Packets

Makes 4 servings

Say "Yum!" to loads of bacon, cheese and chives melted over roasted chunks of potato. Perfect as a side dish for dinner or a satisfying lunch entrée.

Tips

Serve with dollops of sour cream, if desired.

For a tangier flavor, substitute ½ cup (125 mL) crumbled feta or blue cheese for the Cheddar.

- Preheat oven to 375°F (190°C)
- 4 double sheets heavy-duty foil, top sheets sprayed with nonstick cooking spray

3	large potatoes (about 1½ lbs/750 g total), peeled and cut into 1-inch (2.5 cm) cubes	3
1	onion, chopped	1
3 tbsp	freshly grated Parmesan cheese	45 mL
1 tbsp	minced fresh chives	15 mL
1 tsp	seasoning salt	5 mL
¼ tsp	freshly ground black pepper	1 mL
2 tbsp	butter, cut into small pieces	30 mL
½ cup	crumbled cooked bacon	125 mL
½ cup	shredded mozzarella cheese	125 mL
½ cup	shredded Cheddar cheese	125 mL

1. In a large bowl, combine potatoes, onion, Parmesan, chives, seasoning salt and pepper.

2. Divide potato mixture evenly among prepared foil sheets. Dot with butter. Fold foil into flat packets and seal edges tightly. Place packets on a baking sheet.

3. Bake in preheated oven for 15 to 18 minutes, turning packets over once, until potatoes are tender. Carefully, to avoid tearing foil, open packets, allowing steam to escape, and sprinkle evenly with bacon, mozzarella and Cheddar. Reseal packets and bake for 3 to 5 minutes or until cheese is melted.

Dijon Red Potato Salad

If you are looking for a simple, zesty side dish that's perfect for a crowd, this one is a delectable accompaniment for chicken, fish or beef.

Tip

Instead of one large packet, you can make individual servings by dividing the potato mixture evenly among 8 double sheets heavy-duty foil, top sheets sprayed with nonstick cooking spray.

- Preheat oven to 350°F (180°C)
- Triple sheet heavy-duty foil, top sheet sprayed with nonstick cooking spray

½ cup	virgin olive oil	125 mL
⅓ cup	red wine vinegar	75 mL
⅓ cup	Dijon mustard, divided	75 mL
Pinch	freshly ground black pepper	Pinch
2 lbs	red-skinned potatoes, cut into 1-inch (2.5 cm) chunks	1 kg
1	onion, cut into 1-inch (2.5 cm) chunks	1
2 tbsp	chopped fresh parsley	30 mL

1. In a small bowl, whisk together oil, vinegar, 2 tbsp (30 mL) mustard and pepper. Set aside.

2. In a large bowl, toss together potatoes, onions and the remaining mustard.

3. Place prepared foil sheet on a baking sheet. Arrange potato mixture in center of foil. Fold foil into a tent-style packet and seal edges tightly.

4. Bake in preheated oven for 35 to 40 minutes, turning packet over and rotating it occasionally, until potatoes are tender.

5. Remove packet from oven and open with caution, allowing steam to escape. Pour mustard vinaigrette over potato mixture and gently toss to combine. Serve sprinkled with parsley.

Peach Cinnamon Crisp

Makes 4 servings

Sweet, crunchy, gooey and bursting with flavor — these are the best terms to describe this ambrosial dessert.

Tip

Serve with a dollop of whipped cream or a scoop of vanilla ice cream.

- Preheat oven to 325°F (160°C)
- 4 double sheets heavy-duty foil, top sheets sprayed with nonstick cooking spray

½ cup	large-flake (old-fashioned) rolled oats	125 mL
¼ cup	packed brown sugar	60 mL
3 tbsp	finely chopped candied ginger	45 mL
2 tbsp	all-purpose flour	30 mL
1½ tsp	ground cinnamon	7 mL
½ tsp	ground nutmeg	2 mL
¼ cup	cold butter, cut into small pieces	60 mL
4	peaches, sliced	4

1. In a medium bowl, combine oats, brown sugar, ginger, flour, cinnamon and nutmeg. Using a pastry cutter or fork, cut in butter until mixture is crumbly.

2. Divide peaches evenly among prepared foil sheets. Top with oat mixture, dividing evenly. Fold foil into flat packets and seal edges tightly. Place packets on a baking sheet.

3. Bake in preheated oven for 15 to 18 minutes or until peaches are tender.

Roasted Caramel Pecan Pears

Makes 4 servings

All anyone has to say is "caramel" and I am ready to dive right in. If you love caramel too, then you will jump for these pears drizzled with creamy caramel and topped with pecans.

Tips

Bosc, Green Anjou, Bartlett or Comice pears are ideal for this dessert.

- Preheat oven to 325°F (160°C)
- 4 double sheets heavy-duty foil, top sheets sprayed with nonstick cooking spray

4	firm ripe pears (see tip, at left)	4
2 tsp	butter	10 mL
3 tbsp	caramel sauce	45 mL
¼ cup	chopped pecans	60 mL

1. Remove stems from pears, cut pears in half lengthwise and remove cores.

2. For each packet, dot ½ tsp (2 mL) butter in the center of a prepared foil sheet. Drizzle with 1½ tsp (7 mL) caramel sauce. Sprinkle pecans evenly on top of caramel. Place 2 pear halves, cut side down, on top. Drizzle the remaining caramel sauce over pears. Fold foil into flat packets and seal edges tightly. Place packets on a baking sheet.

3. Bake in preheated oven for 15 to 25 minutes or until pears are tender.

4. Invert pears onto dessert plates and drizzle sauce from packets over pears. Serve immediately.

Apple Dumpling Delights

If you have ever fussed with making dumplings, you will be pleasantly surprised by how easily these delightful little dumplings come together to complement the cinnamon apples.

Tips

Firm baking apples, such as Rome or Jonagold, are best suited for this recipe.

For variety, you can substitute dried cranberries for the raisins.

- Preheat oven to 325°F (160°C)
- 4 double sheets heavy-duty foil, top sheets sprayed with nonstick cooking spray

4	large apples (see tip, at left), cut into large chunks	4
¼ cup	raisins	60 mL
2 tsp	ground cinnamon	10 mL
1 tsp	granulated sugar	5 mL
¼ cup	all-purpose baking mix (such as Bisquick)	60 mL

1. Arrange apples in a small mound on each prepared foil sheet, dividing evenly. Sprinkle with raisins, cinnamon and sugar, dividing evenly. Add 1 tbsp (15 mL) baking mix in the center of each packet. Fold foil into flat packets and seal edges tightly. Place packets on a baking sheet.

2. Bake in preheated oven for 30 to 35 minutes or until apples are tender and dumplings have formed and are cooked through.

Index

Library and Archives Canada Cataloguing in Publication

Haugen, Marilyn, author
    150 best recipes for cooking in foil : ovens, BBQ, camping / Marilyn Haugen.

Includes index.
ISBN 978-0-7788-0532-8 (paperback)

    1. Cooking. 2. Aluminum foil. 3. Cookbooks. I. Title. II. Title: One hundred fifty best recipes for cooking in foil.

TX652.H39 2016   641.5   C2016-900310-8